Tips & Tactics for

Marketing
on the
Internet

Edited by Bradford W. Ketchum, Jr.

Inc. Business Resources
Boston, Massachusetts

Published by *Inc.* Business Resources,
a division of Goldhirsh Group, Inc.,
publisher of *Inc.* magazine.
Copyright © 2000 by Goldhirsh Group, Inc.,
Boston, MA
All rights reserved.

No part of this book may be used or reproduced
in any manner whatsoever without written permission
from the publisher. For information, please write:
Permissions Manager, *Inc.* Business Resources,
38 Commercial Wharf, Boston, MA 02110-3883.

Editorial Director: Bradford W. Ketchum, Jr.
Managing Editor: Gail E. Anderson
Text Designer: Martha Abdella

This publication is designed to provide accurate and
authoritative information in regard to the subject matter
covered. However, the publisher is not engaged in rendering
legal, accounting, or other professional advice. If legal
advice or other expert assistance is required, the services
of a competent professional should be sought.

Companies that engage in marketing on the Internet are evolving
rapidly, as are URLs. While every effort has been made to ensure the
accuracy of information in this book, readers should be aware that Web
addresses are subject to change.

This book may be purchased in bulk at discounted rates for sales
promotions, premiums, and fund-raising. Custom copies are also available.
Contact: Custom Publishing Sales Dept.,
Inc. Business Resources, 38 Commercial Wharf,
Boston, MA 02110-3883 (1-800-394-1746).

ISBN 158230-014-3

Second Edition

Printed in the United States of America.

www.inc.com

Contents

Chapter 1   7
Why the Web?
- Clicking on to a market of 35 million to 45 million people.
- Three out of four small businesses report that cost is not a barrier.
- Top reasons for going online: sales, service, and competition.

Chapter 2   11
What's the Tab—and the Return?
- A highly successful site can be launched for less than $400.
- The return doesn't have to be solely financial.
- You don't have to be a computer whiz to manage the Web.
- The three basic steps to launching a site.

Chapter 3   15
Setting Up Your Web Site
- Should you design it yourself or hire an outside Web pro?
- Hosting: the pros and cons of storing your site in-house.
- Questions to ask when shopping for an ISP.
- Three companies share the lessons they learned going online.
- Seven common mistakes to avoid when launching your site.

Chapter 4   21
The ABCs of Online Promotions
- The key to e-mail advertisements.
- Using direct e-mail to attract visitors to your site.
- What you should know about banner ads.
- Marketing to newsgroups: basic tactics for online billboards.

Contents

Chapter 5 25
Five Essentials for Any Site
- It delivers what it promises.
- It takes little time to download.
- Company information is easy to find.
- It's updated frequently.
- It invites user interaction.

Chapter 6 31
Tracking Visitors to Your Site
- What the Web can tell you.
- Web-site tracking software pinpoints visitors.
- Translating hits and clicks.
- Pros and cons of requiring visitors to register.
- Turning data into dollars.

Chapter 7 39
Capsule Cases
For a real-world look at marketing on the Web, here are 41 case histories of companies that are successfully using the Internet in general and the World Wide Web in particular.

CyberSpeak 94
A glossary of 36 terms for dealing with the Internet.

Chapter 1

Why the Web?

Anywhere from 40 million to 60 million people now use the Internet daily. But that statistic can be misleading. Many users are just sending e-mail across the Internet and have never seen the Web or other parts of the Internet, such as the online discussion groups known as newsgroups. As the Web became the marketing buzzword of the late 1990s, researchers and entrepreneurs alike began using statistics on the Internet, Web, and online services interchangeably. It's easy to get confused, so it pays to keep in mind what the Web is and what it's not.

First, the World Wide Web is just a small part of the Internet, with fewer users than the Internet as a whole. How many of the Internet's 66 million users browse the Web? The estimate is somewhere between a half and two-thirds, or 35 million to 45 million. No accurate measuring system exists. But even though the surveys disagree on the exact number of people hooking up, experts agree that the Web is used far more than the commercial online services such as America Online and Prodigy.

Logging on to an online service is not the same as logging on to the Internet. Although all of the online services do connect to the Internet and the Web, they aren't the same as the Web itself. First of all, each online service has its own collection of activities and information that it offers in addition to Internet access. Second, the online services are proprietary networks. This means that every message subscribers send or receive and every site they browse are controlled in some way by administrators. Unlike the Internet, each online service has rules and guidelines about what members can and can't do. Businesses that want to put up sites selling products or services have to negotiate a contract with the online service, often paying exorbitant setup charges and ongoing fees based on a percentage of online sales.

Why the Web?

The number of Web sites doubles every three to five months. As they become easier to use and more graphics-rich, they attract more and more people. By 2002, the Web will have more than 65 million users logging on either through standard Internet access accounts or online services. Web users come from an attractive demographic profile for advertisers—they're likely to be upscale, well-educated, and early technology adopters.

With commercial users logging in at record rates, the Web has quickly become the place to be for business. The rest of the Internet still frowns on commercial activity. Unwary advertisers are rebuffed with harsh "flames," or attacks via e-mail. Most of the users of the rest of the Internet are just chatting with friends or gathering research material. While it's possible to market in some of these areas, for most businesses the Web is the only place to be. Consumers visit the Web to be entertained and to buy. Small businesses are learning how to serve both needs very well.

Internet Users: Business Makes Its Mark

Year	U.S. adults (age 18+) online	Business users
2002	88*	49
2001	78	43
2000	66	36
1999	58	31
1998	48	25

* millions
Source: eMarketer

If your business is not online yet, it soon will be. That's the conclusion that can be drawn from a recent study commissioned by Prodigy Biz Corp., which found that one-third of U.S. small businesses were online. The smallest organizations were the least likely to have taken the plunge. Only one in four companies with fewer than 10 employees reported that it had an Internet pres-

How Small Businesses Use the Web

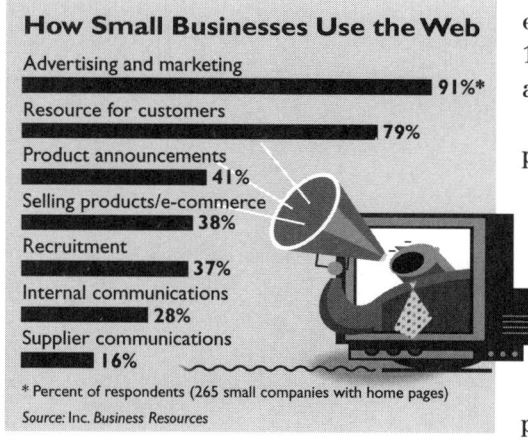

Advertising and marketing: 91%*
Resource for customers: 79%
Product announcements: 41%
Selling products/e-commerce: 38%
Recruitment: 37%
Internal communications: 28%
Supplier communications: 16%

* Percent of respondents (265 small companies with home pages)
Source: Inc. Business Resources

ence, while half of those with 10 or more employees were already online.

Nearly 75% of small companies reported that cost was not a barrier for getting onto the Web. Their biggest hurdle: finding staff to develop and maintain a Web site. The survey results ranked these top four reasons for going online: promoting to prospects (69%); conducting e-commerce (57%); providing better customer service (48%); and competing with other businesses (46%).

Many off-line small businesses planned to get online in 2000. Some 40% of businesses that didn't have Web sites—approximately 2.1 million—said they would be online within a few months.

The New Yorker once ran a cartoon of two dogs sitting in front of a computer. One is typing while he tells the other, "On the Internet, nobody knows you're a dog." On the Web, nobody knows you're a small business. The difference between a bad Web site and a good one isn't money, it's creativity. Creative, flexible sites attract the most visitors, who then tell their business colleagues and friends to have a look. Setting up a good Web site isn't expensive, so small-company sites can look just as good, or better, than large-company sites. On the Web, taking chances and moving quickly pays off. ∎

Chapter 2

What's the Tab—and the Return?

Your Web site should be an integral part of your marketing strategy, with specific goals for measuring its success. Say, for example, a catalog company rents a particular mailing list. The company hopes for a 3% return on the highly qualified, expensive list. If the list doesn't deliver the desired return on investment, the company won't make the same bad investment twice.

Every company should do the same thing with its Web page. Once you know the costs of setting up your Web site, establish a goal for your return on investment. The goal should reflect three considerations: What kind of return is desired? How will it be measured? And over what period?

The type of return doesn't have to be solely financial—in the form of a certain percentage of total sales by a particular date. It could be to gather a number of names for a mailing list, or to cut mailing or telephone expenses by a certain amount after handing over some customer service functions to the Web site. Perhaps the company hopes to cut marketing expenses, while still posting the same sales growth percentages. Whatever it is, the return should be set up to measure the main focus of the Web site. For example, you probably wouldn't want to focus on hiring a certain percentage of employees from Web-site applications if it's a catalog site. It would be more to the point to measure sales instead. In the beginning, choose one main aspect to measure. If that goes well, it's easy to add more areas to evaluate.

Once the type of return is established, make sure there is a way to measure it and that systems are in place to do it. Web sales can easily be measured at a site that handles online transactions. But how would you measure the portion of decreased mailing expenses attributable to the Web site? How would you decide if customer service functions are successful on the Web (perhaps by looking for decreased telephone costs, or a certain number of existing customers signing up for online support packages)? It's important to take the time up front to establish clear guidelines for measuring the site's success or failure, so that there can be no question once the site goes live (see Chapter 6, page 31, for tips on how to measure traffic at your Web site).

When the site opens, start measuring how well it performs. Talk to other companies that have had sites up for a while. Ask how they evaluate their sites and what their timetable is for turning a profit.

Going online not only broadens your reach and market potential; it also promises significant cost savings. The nature of the Net and the sheer volume of users, for example, can greatly reduce the cost and time it takes to acquire each new customer. Web-based answers to frequently asked questions (FAQs) can save time spent answering repetitive inquiries about your products and services (e.g., store and office locations, hours, product descriptions, and return policies). The capacity for cost savings should be a major consideration in comparing your investment and return.

You don't have to be a computer whiz to build and manage a successful Web site, nor do you have to make a huge investment. Not counting the cost of back-office operations for e-commerce (e.g., order processing, billing, fulfillment, and post-sale service), which vary widely by industry, successful small-business sites have been launched for less than $400, including domain name registration ($75), Internet access ($30), software ($200), and set-up ($50). There are three basic steps:

1. *Get Internet access.* An Internet service provider (ISP) will give you access to the Net through a phone line. (Be sure the access number is a local call, not a toll call.) The basic service will cost about $20 to $50 a month. America Online (AOL), AT&T WorldNet, and Microsoft Network (MSN) are among the leading national ISPs. For a list of access providers, visit

www.isps.com, which will allow you to search a database of more than 4,000 ISPs by area code.

2. *Put software to work.* You'll need a browser, such as Netscape Navigator and Communicator or Microsoft Internet Explorer, that allows you to view pages on the Web from your computer screen. (For a listing of browsers, visit **www.browsers. com**.) You'll also need software that will help you establish a professional presence on the Net. Among the most popular programs are Claris Home Page 3.0 ($99; **www.claris.com**) and Microsoft FrontPage 2000 ($149; **www.microsoft.com/frontpage**). Some ISPs, including AOL and EarthLink, provide one free Web site per account, along with simple fill-in-the-blank templates to build the site.

> **Menu of ROI Metrics**
> - Gains in sales and profits
> - Number of new accounts
> - Market penetration
> - Reduced costs (phone, postage, literature, market research, support)
> - Cost per qualified lead
> - Time savings
> - Percentage of customers accessing the Web site
> - Impact on turnover

3. *Hire a host.* You can use your ISP as your Web host or retain a hosting service that can provide specific functions that your business may need for e-commerce. Many Web-site hosts provide free templates and tools for building a site. Some include Web design and promotion as part of their package. And others offer management services and e-commerce support. Web hosts normally charge about $20 to $50 a month. In exchange, you'll receive technical support 24 hours a day. For a small business just getting its feet wet on the Web, consider a Web-hosting service that offers a basic site with the option to move up to a more advanced one as you learn to manage the site. For a directory of hosts, visit **www.hostsearch.com**, which includes a list of e-commerce hosting services, such as catalog.com, ValueWeb, and WebHosting.com. ■

Chapter 3

Setting Up Your Web Site

Should you design your Web site yourself or hand it off to a professional Web designer? The advantage of tackling the job yourself is that you maintain control and can make instant changes without worrying about cost. Software programs such as Macromedia Dreamweaver (www.macromedia.com), NetObjects Fusion (www.netobjects.com), and Microsoft FrontPage (www.microsoft.com) have point-and-click interfaces that are designed for non-programmers. Using one of these, you should be able to have a Web page up and running in a day or two.

For many small businesses, however, outsourcing site design is the preferred option. "For us, the question of design was simple. I lacked the knowledge, so instead of spending time learning, I wanted to do what I do best, and that's sell real estate," says Carl W. Riese, principal of Segal Riese Realtors, in West Islip, N.Y. (www.westisliphomes.com). Riese's decision to use an outside Web designer paid off. "We had our site up and running in a matter of weeks, and there's not much cost for site management because the only thing we change regularly are our house listings," he says.

Good designers have the tools and know-how to do a great job, but Web design services can be costly, and the skills of designers vary greatly. Be sure to screen the designer's work and check references.

Before you start designing your Web site, you have to decide where to store it: in-house or with an Internet service provider (ISP). Storing a Web site in-house is more expensive but can be smarter over the long run. When the computer your Web site is on is just down the hall, it's cheaper and faster to experiment with the site's capabilities. You can change, update, and expand the site at will. If you want to gather customer feedback, update price listings, and tweak the site as your company grows, you can do so more quickly and economically with an in-house server.

You can also link the site directly to other company resources—sales, inventory, or customer service applications, for example. If a visitor to your site suddenly decides to order 1,000 units on the spot, the on-site server can link the sale directly to your order-processing software.

Like any important management decision, creating a Web site to be stored in-house requires planning. Decide who's going to maintain the system—an employee, an outside contractor, or some combination of the two? Someone needs to be on call at all times so that a crashed system gets back online as quickly as possible. Consider timing, too. Exploding demand has created backlogs for the phone companies. Plan accordingly—there may be a waiting list for installing the dedicated line you'll need to connect part of the Internet backbone.

If you do opt for an outside service, keep these six points in mind as you shop for an ISP:

1. *Does the ISP provide the basic services you need, such as e-mail, newsgroups, and file transfer protocol (FTP)?* If you're going online solely to get customer feedback, e-mail alone may be enough. But if you want to ship reports to satellite offices, your provider will have to offer FTP.

2. *How good is its technical support?* Your business must have someone who understands your special needs. If they can't help you, then it doesn't matter if it offers support 24 hours a day, seven days a week.

3. *Does it offer the bandwidth, or speed of Internet access, that's most appropriate for your business?* If you have large groups of employees who'll be using the connection simultaneously, you need more bandwidth. And you'll need an ISP that itself has high-speed connection to the Internet.

4. *Is the price right?* Most services fall within the $20 to $40 per month

range. Expect to pay more if you need high bandwidth and more than just basic service.

5. *How many POP, or remote connection, sites does the ISP have?* If you or your employees travel a lot for business, a nearby POP provides Internet access at the price of a local phone call.

6. *Can it help you set up and maintain a Web page?* Some ISPs only host, or store, sites. If the provider doesn't offer design expertise, it should be able to recommend someone who does.

Lessons learned going online. Everyone has heard about the dotcom companies that post a Web site and laugh all the way to their IPOs. But what about the companies whose Web sites don't produce as expected? The managers of three existing small companies who let their preconceived notions stand in the way, share valuable lessons about how *not* to translate a business onto the Web. All three companies are still online, but wiser after their startup experiences.

1. *Bells and whistles don't always work.* Three years ago, Rick Edler of the Edler Group (**www.edlergroup.com**), a real estate agency in Palos Verdes, Calif., posted a low-tech Web site, basically a glorified business card. But Edler wanted more, so he hired a Web developer to deliver the latest technical gimmicks. Graphics spun all over the screen as testimonials from happy clients scrolled up and down. The first site cost $285. This one cost $7,000.

But it took too long to download, and traffic was disappointing. "So much was happening," Edler says. "We were scaring people away."

Then the Webmaster disappeared. Edler was appalled to learn that he wasn't authorized to make changes on his own site. He couldn't even update property listings. To seize control, Edler literally had to scrap the site. For $2,000 he built a third, simpler version. It has links to Realtor.com and Bamboo.com where buyers can check listings or take a video house tour. But no more razzle-dazzle.

Edler admits that marketing glitz diverted him from the true function of his site. "We started out generating leads," Edler says. "Now our Internet site is the last thing our clients go to, not the first. It helps us close sales, but it doesn't try to make our cold calls for us."

2. *The traffic myth: "Hits" equal sales.* A few years after he founded Blue Marlin, a company that sells vintage baseball caps and apparel, CEO Erik Stuebe was seduced by the Internet. A Web developer told him that online sales could represent as much as 20% of the company's revenues in just three years. So Stuebe plunked down $35,000 to launch **www.bluemarlincorp.com**. Like Edler, Stuebe wanted, and got, an action-packed site, designed as a baseball-history-lover's paradise, rich with lore and special effects. Deeper into the site, visitors could buy Blue Marlin's products.

People flocked to visit, but hits do not equal sales. By the end of 1998, Stuebe had sold only $50,000 worth of merchandise online. So he plowed more money into the Web site for more updates and features. Finally, in 1999, Web-based sales started to show signs of life, reaching $120,000. But this still represents a small portion of the company's revenues. Now Stuebe is more careful about how much he spends on the site and is diverting more funds back into his wholesale business, where customers can touch and feel his wares.

3. *Share the passion—but only to a point.* Daniel Harrison's Poolandspa.com (formerly Paramount Services), a Long Island, N.Y., pool and hot-tub supply company has been on the Web longer than Amazon.com. When chat rooms and message boards started to become centers of passionate customer interaction, Harrison thought an online community would also work for him.

So he paid $2,500 for the software, and his ISP installed the technology on Poolandspa.com's site (**www.poolandspa.com**). Harrison promoted the new community on the main pages of his site and offered a 10% discount on all products bought during a scheduled, live online chat. But at the appointed hour, just 10 people came to the party. Undaunted, Harrison figured it was just a matter of time. However, the next scheduled live chat yielded only six people.

The company was receiving "a tremendous amount" of e-mail from customers, says Harrison, so he thought he could translate e-mail to chat. Always willing to try the next new technology, Harrison says he followed the AOL model for chat, but without one key ingredient. AOL was featuring celebrity hosts—a big draw. Harrison was trying to make an event out of something with less glamour. And he wasn't meeting his customers' needs.

"If the hot-tub water is turning your kid's hair green, you don't want to wait for the answer until [the live chat] Wednesday night at 10," he quips. "My customers don't want to talk to each other. If they have a question, they want to talk to an expert."

Poolandspa.com still offers online visitors the opportunity to chat, but Harrison now understands the role of a chat on his site. It has been useful, he says, for customer interaction and customer recommendations about Poolandspa.com's products and their use.

The three lessons above help underscore the pitfalls involved in setting up a Web site and trying to drive traffic to it. Here's a summary of the most common mistakes to avoid as you launch your site:

Lack of clarity. Less is more. Sure, you want to say lots about your business, but your home page should be clean and concise, providing just enough information to attract visitors (e.g., company name, address, phone number, and a brief description of exactly what you do). As with any type of advertising, it's important that your home page let the Web surfer know exactly what you do and that every other element of the site promotes its basic purpose.

Clutter. It may be tempting to use special effects, but the best tactic for a small-business site is discretion. Do not cram your home page with Web gimcrackery, promotional plugs, and pointless animation. Pages that are graphics-heavy are slow to load, and that can be frustrating for viewers. Web designers operate under the principle that users will wait no more than five seconds before thinking about moving to another site.

Bad navigation. Navigating your site should be easy and consistent. Give visitors something to click on upon arrival—do not force them to scroll. Rule of thumb: Offer no more than five to seven navigation buttons per Web page. Make sure each page has a navigation bar allowing browsers to move around without going back to the home page. But, they should always be able to go to the home page if they want to.

Going live too early. It pays big dividends to beta-test your site before publicizing it. Even Amazon.com, the online bookstore considered a leading e-commerce model, conducted a three-month dry run to work out the bugs before opening to the public.

Poor marketing. With so many Web sites, it's increasingly difficult to get noticed. To make it worse, search engines change their algorithms (sequences of steps for programming computers to solve specific problems) almost weekly, so you have to keep learning new tricks to outsmart them and make your listing rise to the top. Thus, you need a crack team to keep experimenting with links, banners, and META tags (key words or descriptions used by search engines to categorize your site).

Failure to respond to e-mail. You have to check e-mail from customers with the same regularity that you check for voice mail—i.e., at least twice a day. And, you have to respond, or people won't come back.

Insecure transactions. The biggest mistake you can make is to offer credit-card transactions that are not secure. If you say, "Print out the form and fax it," you're asking people not to buy. ∎

Chapter 4

The ABCs of Online Promotions

The key to any site's success is traffic. No company can make sales, advertise, offer customer service, or charge advertisers unless people visit the Web site—and they don't necessarily come just because you build it. Your site has to be promoted so that Web users can find it among the increasing number of sites. This doesn't mean launching a high-powered and expensive ad campaign. One of the great advantages of the Web for small businesses is that it's inexpensive—often free—to let people know that a site is open and where it is. Here are the best ways to get the word out after opening a Web site:

E-mail advertisements. Most e-mail programs allow users to create small files of text that automatically append to the bottom of every e-mail message they send. For example, at the end of each e-mail message, you can say something like, "XYZ Company, meeting your real estate needs since 1964." The file is called a "signature," and any company with a Web site should include the URL and a brief description of the site in key employees' signature files. Thus, every e-mail sent could also include a brief ad like, "Visit our Web site at www.newproperty.com to play Land on Boardwalk!"

The key to an effective signature file is to keep it short, ideally four lines or fewer. Some people create very elaborate signature files, drawing little pictures or quoting long passages from books or poems. This type of file just takes up space, and nobody bothers to read the whole thing after the first time. But a short file usually gets glanced at every time, prompting them to remember the message.

Direct e-mail. If your company's site is set up to collect e-mail addresses of visitors, add a question next to that section asking if they'd mind receiving e-mail notifying them of changes to your Web site, or changes in the industry, or changes and updates to whatever key information your site offers. Once armed with a list of users willing to receive e-mail, start sending it to them. Don't abuse their trust by overwhelming them with press releases every time a minor change is made to the site, but do put together a regular mailer, perhaps once a month, pointing out a few new products available on the site or key issues discussed there. The mailer shouldn't steal the site's thunder. It should be more of a teaser designed to make readers want to visit the site. Keep it very short and current. (For details on how one company leverages its electronic list, check Case No. 19, on page 63.)

Banner ads. These are the main forms of advertising on the Internet. They are rectangular ads (hence, "banners") placed on other companies' search engines, chat rooms, online magazines, and Web sites. Banners can be purchased on portal sites for as little as $2 per 1,000 page views. One caveat: The click-through rate is often as low as 2%. However, a recent Andersen Consulting study shows that experienced Web users are more likely to buy online after exposure to banner ads than they are after exposure to traditional advertising. Consider exchanging banners, too (see Case 18, page 62). If you can live with the look of another company's ad on your home page, you can post your banner on its site. Search in your browser under "banner exchange" for free exchange services.

Online billboards. A collection of Internet discussion groups, known as "newsgroups," works like bulletin boards—people can post messages on certain topics. Anyone who visits the newsgroup can read all of the past messages and also post messages themselves. There are more than 20,000 newsgroups, each focusing on a specific topic, such as pet health care, foreign car repair, Web-page development, computers for sale, or fan clubs for rock musicians. This area of the Internet is notoriously noncommercial, and users hate posted advertisements. Despite this, some companies do market to newsgroups successfully. Here are four basic approaches:

1. *The first essential tactic is to focus only on newsgroups where your company's product or service is of interest.* Alberto Martin of Alberto's Nightclub (see page 63) only posts messages in alternative and Latin music newsgroups, for example, where he thinks the majority of readers are in his target demographic.

2. *The second tactic is to read the messages posted there for several weeks before posting your own.* Perhaps that particular group is violently opposed to any marketing, no matter how soft-pedaled—it's better to find out before posting a message than after.

3. *Post very brief messages, making clear in the subject line of the message what the topic is.* For example, listing the subject as "Great opportunity to save!" marks that message clearly as an advertisement, begging for angry e-mail in response. But listing "Info on new nonstick cookware," makes the subject clear. Those who don't want to know about the cookware won't read the message, and therefore won't respond with vitriolic e-mail.

4. *Be honest about who you are—someone from a company trying to sell a product or service.* Writing "I work for a company that sells Ketchum Klean Soap, and here's how to reach us if you're interested," will be more respected in newsgroups than writing "I've used Ketchum Klean Soap and love it. E-mail me if you'd like to know more." Keep those messages short, avoiding hyperbole. Since many users are paying by the hour to access the Internet, they don't like to waste time online.

Some companies first post messages in the target newsgroups, asking if the participants would mind their messages. For example, in a sports newsgroup a company might post a message saying, "Would people here be interested in occasional information on new shoe technology?" Often, many users are, and they will respect a company for asking. ∎

Chapter 5

Five Essentials for Any Site

Once users find a site—through a search engine, by reading a URL in a magazine ad, or by being sent to the site from a link on another site—there are certain things they'll expect to see no matter what. Ignoring these important elements will mark any site as amateurish and not worth visiting again:

It delivers what it promises. Say a Web user types "car repair" into a search engine, and AutoMile Car Dealership turns up among the sites that list "car repair" in their keyword sections. That site had better have more than just a line reading, "Our repair shop is open 12 hours a day," to justify listing "repair" in the keyword section. Otherwise, that user will be angry to have wasted the time visiting the site, only to learn there's no information on car repair there. Make sure that a keyword leads a user to a sizable amount of information at your site about the requested topic.

It doesn't take long to download. The classic mistake that many companies make is to include a large photo or sound or video clip on the Web site. The problem is, graphics and sound take a long time to download compared to text. For a Web user with an older 28.8 modem, waiting several minutes for something to download is bound to make the user run away from the site. Many interesting visual effects can be created that don't take long to download. For example, skinny horizontal graphics that stretch across the screen take shorter time to download than large ones that use a lot of vertical space. Black-and-white graphics load faster than colored ones.

Company information is easy to find. On the Web, it doesn't matter if a company is in Maine or Maryland. With a click of the mouse, it's just as easy for Web users to reach one as it is the other. But nobody is living completely in cyberspace yet. Users want to know where the companies are in the real world. Perhaps the customer lives near the company and would like to visit, or maybe they'd just find it interesting to know that a cactus greenhouse is located in Vermont. It's essential to place the Web site somewhere in traditional real-world space, so always list a physical company location. Even more essential is to include an address, as well as phone and fax numbers. Some Web users want to call a company or mail in an order rather than e-mail it. Usually this information provides reassurance that the site belongs to a real company and not a con artist. Sometimes the Web user just wants the information because he or she is more comfortable with traditional contact methods.

It's updated frequently. Most Web site administrators update their sites at least once a week. This time-intensive task consumes a lot of labor, especially when the One-Hour Browse Rule is factored into the equation: For every change made to the site, the person making the change should browse the Web for at least one hour. Keeping the site "fresh" is key for companies that expect visitors to return. There is so much action on the Web that it's tempting for visitors to jump somewhere more exciting if your company's site bores them.

There's user interaction. One of the big advantages of this medium is that it allows users to interact immediately. They can send e-mail, fill out a form, enter a contest, or request information the instant they have the urge. And they expect to be asked—it's part of the fun and entertainment of browsing the Web. A site with no "user feedback" e-mail forms, no games to play, or no forms to fill out is a site that will soon sit untapped.

One kind of interactive element some sites can include is a piece of software that will search a product database by keyword. For example, customers at a bicycle retailer Web site can type in "mountain bike locks" to get a list of the desired products. This internal search engine saves time compared to browsing an entire list of products or even the list of all bicycle locks. Customers appreciate that and are more likely to revisit that site rather than other bicycle retailer sites.

Another interactive and time-saving piece of software is an online form. It can be used by visitors requesting company or product information, registering to visit the site, asking for specific customer service, or signing up for a customized e-mail newsletter. The form can even be structured so that the Web user can customize the page itself. By expressing preferences in an online form, the user can specify which parts of the Web site will show and which will be hidden on the next visit.

Web sites have copied another part of the Internet—the live "chat." On some sites, visitors can click on a button to go to a screen, or "room," where there is a list of the other visitors who are present at the same time. Anytime someone types a sentence and hits the "enter" key on the keyboard, everyone in the "chat room" instantly sees that person's name and the message and can respond. However, it can be difficult to draw visitors regularly to these chat areas. What frequently happens is someone will go to visit one, but because nobody else is there, the visitor quickly leaves. The smart approach is to schedule dis-

Top Five Reasons Visitors Return to Web Sites

High-quality content
75%

Easy to use
66%

Downloads quickly
58%

Updated frequently
54%

Coupons and incentives
14%

Source: Forrester Research (poll of 8,600 online households)

cussions on specific topics and then publicize them, so that enough people attend at the same time to be able to carry on a conversation.

Whether to include certain elements in a Web site is still being debated. For example, should a Web site be debuted before it's really finished? At an unfinished site, users who click on the unfinished section see a small "under construction" sign. Some Web users hate it and won't return to a site that's under construction, especially if they do revisit once and it's still under construction. But some users don't seem to mind. "Under construction" sites still receive visitors. Some Web developers claim it can be a smart marketing move, because it piques the interest of visitors who figure that an unfinished Web site is worth revisiting to see how it turns out.

For companies that decide to gamble on rolling out an unfinished site, there are two rules to follow: First, most of the site must be finished. Second, put a date on the unfinished section so visitors know when to expect completion. Otherwise, after returning several times to an "under construction" site that shows no signs of ever being finished, they'll give up.

A clever site will attract visitors who will return regularly to see what's new. One trick that you can use to encourage revisiting is to program a short warning message to flash on the computer screen when users click on an external link. That message might say something like, "You're leaving our site now. Save the URL so you can come back easily." Users can then choose to save the Web-site address in their browser software's memory by just pulling down the "save" option on the menu bar. This is called "bookmarking," and it saves users from having to remember long, awkward URLs of the sites they visit often. Instead, they just select a site from the bookmarked list on the browser, and the software remembers the URL.

While they're browsing the site, users may buy something. But if there is no sale, how does your company know that anyone has stopped by? It's not as if it were a real store, where the proprietor can see at any given moment how many customers have come in. No, it's better than that—Web-site operators can collect more information than store owners can. How many people stop in during any given time period? Where do they come from, how long do they stay, and what do they look at? The next chapter explains the many different ways that you can track all of that information. ■

The One-Minute Web Test

Once you have a Web site up and running, this one-minute test can help you spot potential problems before they take a toll on your online traffic. If your answer is yes to these 10 questions, your Web site's a winner!

❑ Do my Web pages load quickly?
❑ Is it immediately apparent what my company does or sells?
❑ Is my menu viewable and easy to navigate?
❑ Does my site look attractive when viewed with different browsers?
❑ Are colors and graphic elements consistent on all pages?
❑ Are my company's address, phone number, and e-mail address easily accessible?
❑ Is my site free of unnecessary gimmicks and graphics?
❑ Does my site offer valuable information?
❑ Does my site reflect my commitment to quality?
❑ Would I want to do business with my company?

Site Essentials

Chapter 6

Tracking Visitors to Your Site

Let's assume that you set up an attractive Web site, following all the tips and tricks for getting visitors to come early and often. You hope to build an electronic mailing list and make sales to a certain percentage of your visitors. But how will you gather those e-mail addresses? And how will you know what part of the site visitors find the most interesting? Or which part compels visitors to make a purchase? One wonderful thing about the Web is that simple software programs exist to gather all of this information.

When advertising in traditional media, it's often impossible to accurately track customer response. When Bob's Cigar Shop takes out an advertisement in the local newspaper, nobody knows how many readers actually look at that ad or for how long. If Bob polls every walk-in customer, asking where they learned about his shop, he'll only get a rough idea of how many are making purchases based on his ad. If Bob wants to analyze his ad statistically, he'll have to invest a lot of time calculating how many readers the newspaper says it has, how many customers said they made a purchase in his store after seeing the ad, and the average amount of those purchases. It's hardly an exact science.

What the Web can tell you. Telesales organizations and catalogers have long tracked what advertisement customers are responding to by asking them, "Where did you hear about us?" or asking for an identification number from the catalog. But the problem with this method is the same one that Bob has—many customers don't remember or care. Since they're supplying the information, it will often be flawed, because customers forget where they learned about the company. Customers ordering through someone else's catalog, or ordering without a catalog, further skew the information.

But on the Web, customers are tracked accurately without even knowing it. As a company with a Web site, you can find out how many people visit your site, where they come from (another Web site that linked them to your site? a search engine?), how long they stay, what sections they browse, and for how long. If you ask visitors to the site to fill out a simple registration form, you can also tell who's a new visitor and who's a repeat visitor. Plus, you can gather demographic information that is essential if you want to sell space on your Web site to advertisers. Advertisers want to know how long visitors stay during each visit, if the same visitors are returning again and again, what sections they're looking at and for how long, and what type of access they have (through a corporate account, government organization, or university). Advertisers pay for Web advertising using the same model as companies that pay for magazine or newspaper ads—prices are based on how many people read the publication.

Web-site tracking software can gather significantly more detailed information about readers than any newspaper or magazine can offer. Print publications can only give the number of subscribers and newsstand sales, not the number of actual readers each month. With Web tracking software, every company with a site can track how many people look at the site each day.

There are basically two ways of tracking visitors using software. The first dates back to the early days of the Web: A typical person visiting a Web site clicks on a page, enlarges a graphic, listens to a Web audio recording, leaves, and then comes back and makes other moves within the site. Each of those activities makes a request of the Web site's host computer to send the visitor's computer some electronic information. Those requests are tracked as "hits." Basically, a hit registers each time a visitor clicks on part of the site. A hit also registers for each graphic or link on a page. So if a visitor merely looks at a page with four graphics on it, that visitor registers as four hits. And if a visitor arrives at a particular site, then clicks on four different pages, plays a short video clip, gets disconnected, and comes back and clicks on two more pages before leaving, that particular visit registers at least 10 hits to the server software.

A site that claims 10,000 hits a week may in reality only have 2,000 visitors a week, each one clicking around the site five times before leaving. Or it could have 8,000 visitors a week, but most only look at the site's first page before leaving. Companies rely on various calculations for translating their hit rates into number of visitors, but, again, it's not an exact science.

If the information is unreliable, why do companies still use it? One reason is that the capability to track hit rates is already programmed into server software, so Web-site developers don't have to buy extra software. Free software is also available on the Web for companies that want a separate software package offering a bit more detail than provided by some server software. Rather than buy a complex software package or pay an ISP to track the information, companies using hit rates can simply rely on their server software or download the free software to get a general idea of the site's traffic and trend information.

The data is saved in files, which can then be reviewed on screen or printed out. If a Web site's server has a monitor attached to it, someone sitting at that computer can watch the hit-rate information being gathered: If three people are looking at the site, the monitor would show columns of data that track the visitors' progress through the pages. That information can be collected into a report as often as the company wants—daily, weekly, or most common, monthly. Some tracking reports are stored in a form compatible with database software, so they can be analyzed more easily. You can set up hit-rate data files to show whatever information, in whichever order, you choose.

Tracking Visitors

33

10 Ways to Build Customer Affinity

Web sites grow stale if not updated frequently. Novelty builds customer affinity and repeat business. While a periodic redesign never hurts, there are simpler and less expensive ways to keep your site fresh:

1. Highlight new products or services.
2. Advertise "Internet-only" specials.
3. Cycle through facts or information of interest to your clientele.
4. Continually add features to your site, along with the word *new* on the navigation buttons that link to those features.
5. Toot your own horn. Post brief press releases, publish the number of customers served to date, announce a big job just acquired or finished, reprint stories about your company.
6. Post the day's date on your home page.
7. Arrange for, and emphasize, fresh links to other sites.
8. Conduct a contest or weekly survey.
9. Offer a "tip of the week."
10. Change graphics or photos often.

Some companies have adapted hit-rate tracking software to offer even more detailed information. In addition to hit rates, they can determine what browser software visitors are using, what site the user just came from (so a company can judge how many visitors come from a link from another site), what modem speed the visitors are using (so the company can put fewer graphics on the site if most visitors are using very slow modems, for example), and what type of Internet access accounts visitors have (commercial access or from a university or government organization).

The software will also track error messages. For example, if the computer is overloaded when a visitor tries to play a video clip, and the visitor gets an error message saying that the clip is currently unavailable, the company sees that message on the hit-rate log. So the company will know if there's a peak time when lots of error messages go out and can look for problems with the site's capability. Even with this additional data, a company that talks about visitors in terms of hit rates is still working with very vague information.

With either type of traffic tracking, the names and e-mail addresses of the visitors themselves usually remain anonymous unless they voluntarily provide it. If visitors provide that, they might also be willing to provide demographic information about themselves, such as where they live, their income level, and a few details about their family's purchasing decisions. Gathering this data at Web sites is becoming more common as the Web grows. Companies need this information because it helps them focus the site to visitors' demographic profiles. E-mail addresses are important because mailing lists are valuable as a way to attract repeat visitors and recruit new ones by word of mouth.

Some companies require visitors to register before they can even access the site. Basically, it works like this: Visitors to the site see an introductory page showing what information and entertainment the site offers. On that page, a notice explains that in order for advertisers to continue to sponsor the site, or in order for the company to customize the site to visitors upon their return, registration is necessary before the visitor can delve further. At that point, visitors can either leave or continue with the registration process.

The registration form is typically only a page or two and usually doesn't ask for full names and mailing addresses. Most Web users don't want to provide that much personal information. Instead, surveys ask for general information like age, interests, income, and family statistics. Once the form is filled out, visitors get a password to access the site.

The first company to require visitors to register was *Wired* magazine at its Web site, HotWired (**www.hotwired.com**), in 1994. Visitors who registered

Tracking Visitors

35

were issued passwords to access the site. To return, visitors had to remember those passwords to gain entry to the site. HotWired was able to gather tracking information on repeat visitors—what they browsed at the site and how often they returned. The magazine used that data to become one of the first Web sites to sell advertising, making thousands of dollars per month from advertisers like Audi and setting a Web money-making precedent.

The biggest risk to registering visitors is that they may decide just to skip the site altogether rather than fill out the form. Many Web users dislike being tracked and will boycott sites that try. It's also very easy for visitors to throw off statistics, and they gleefully do just that. At sites that require registration in exchange for a password, visitors fake their demographic information. Knowing that they're being tracked, they click on information they don't really want. And once they leave, they give their password to others. For some time, HotWired's most popular visitor was "cypherpunk," a name linked to a password passed among countless users. That name topped HotWired's hit list month after month.

Another risk to requiring visitors to register is that the data isn't completely accurate. Since visitors are volunteering the information, they're likely to make something up when faced with a question like, "How many times in the past year have you bought copier paper?" To get the most accurate results, keep the form simple and short.

It's not difficult to imagine how useful this tracking information can be. Imagine placing an ad in a wide-circulation magazine or newspaper. Imagine that every time somebody looks at that ad, a database tracks what they do. It tracks what the person looked at right before the ad, which tells whether the placement of the ad is successful. It tracks how long they looked at the ad and what parts of the ad they read, which tells how compelling the ad is. And it tracks what the person does immediately after looking at the ad, if they have taken action in response to it. This kind of information can help drive a company's marketing decisions and product research. Gathering visitor feedback via e-mail supplements this information. Companies have even set up virtual roundtables with customers online to discuss future products or services or gather feedback on existing ones.

Tracking information can also work for a site immediately, before the company even sees the printouts. That information can be automatically tied to advertising at the site, whether those ads are for the site's products and services or for sponsors. Here's how the process works: A visitor to a real estate company's site fills out an online form asking for information about vacation property on Cape Cod. After clicking on the form and receiving in return a list of brokers or properties for sale in that area, the visitor might also see an ad for a mortgage company that specializes in vacation property financing or an ad for a vacation time-share association. If the visitor clicks on those links for more information, the real estate company can track that process and show the mortgage company just how many visitors are being sent to them. That's one way to establish the value of those ads.

Data turns into dollars. Not only is Web-site tracking information useful, but it's essential for companies that want to make money on the Web. Is your company ready to profit from marketing on the Web? While it's important to learn as much about the medium as you can before investing in it, that doesn't mean you should wait until Web advertising becomes as popular and costly as a 30-second spot on Super Bowl Sunday before you test the waters. With the cost of Web sites so low and the size of the potential market so huge, it will pay to jump in and get your feet wet now.

For insights into smaller businesses that have taken the plunge, check the 41 case histories on the following pages. All of the companies are successfully using the Internet in general and the World Wide Web in particular. ■

Capsule Cases

Identity
Page

1. I Before E, Except After C.com — 40
2. You Are Your URL — 41
3. Addresses: Making Your Second Choice Fly — 43
4. Making Your URL Ubiquitous — 44
5. Listing with Search Engines — 45

Content

6. Siting Your Information — 46
7. Quick Game Gets 'em to Click — 47
8. Bells and Whistles: Fun vs. Function — 48
9. Buzz Lures Repeat Traffic — 49
10. Disk Jockey Tunes In to Online Lessons — 50
11. Web's Next Killer App: Arugula? — 53
12. Not Every Business Begets a Cult — 55

Marketing

13. Sell Yourself with Your Signature — 56
14. Retailer Retools Its Competitive Edge — 57
15. Web Sites Work for Mom and Pop, Too — 59
16. E-newsletter Clicks with Buyers — 60
17. Target Marketing via E-zines — 61
18. Banner Exchange: Test for Free — 62
19. Nightclub Swings with 100-page Site — 63
20. Selling Links to Your Site — 65

Page

21. Giving Birth to National Sales — 66
22. Web Acrobatics — 67
23. Clocks Click in Antique Network — 68
24. Setting Up Shop in a Cybermall — 69

Customer Support & Feedback

25. Add Cybervalue to Your Proposal — 70
26. Dreamboats Set Sale on the Web — 71
27. Add 'Net Value for Customers — 73
28. Community Builds Repeat Business — 74
29. Tracking 3,000 Visitors Daily — 75
30. Promoting in Newsgroups — 76
31. Need Opinion on New Item? Go Online — 77
32. Web Widens Legal Boundaries — 78
33. Useful Info Gets Site Seers to Sign In — 79
34. Freebies Entice Surfers to Sign On — 80

E-commerce

35. Giving Consumers Five Ways to Buy — 81
36. E-commerce Recipe Evolves Over Time — 82
37. How a Hot-Sauce Shop Sells Online — 85
38. Branding Is Fine, but Selling Is Better — 87
39. Lessons from the Links — 89
40. Party of 10? Click Here — 91
41. To Grow Sales, Think "Niche Knack" — 93

Case 1

I Before E, Except After C.com

Poor spelling, as your fourth-grade teacher may have warned you, always comes back to haunt you. But Jim Kelly was shocked to discover just how serious the problem could be for his business.

The owner and founder of Rejuvenation Lamp & Fixture Co., a lighting maker in Portland, Oreg., was losing up to 25% of potential customers simply because they couldn't spell his company's name. Customers have been addressing letters to "Rejuvination" since Kelly founded the company, in 1977. But the common mistake never got in the way of business. That is, not until 1997, when the company launched a Web site, (**www.rejuvenation.com**).

When several customers told Kelly they couldn't find his site, he began to suspect that the problem was phonetic. So he registered a second domain name, (**www.rejuvination.com**), and posted a link to his real site on it. If you can't beat 'em, he reasoned, why not join 'em?

By monitoring the site's traffic, Kelly has learned that a full quarter of his visitors type in the misspelled URL and arrive at the correct destination through the link. Although the solution was effective, Kelly would have preferred to avoid the confusion. "Next time I start a company, its name will be short, sweet, and easy to spell," he says. "Brite Lites would have been good." ∎

Case 2

You Are Your URL

To do business on the Web, you'll want to choose a great domain name. Unfortunately, that may not be as easy as you think. Many entrepreneurs have run into trouble after discovering that someone else has beaten them to the name-registering punch. Others have problems keeping their URLs when someone challenges their right to use a particular name. This sort of wrangle has plagued companies both big and small. In most cases, there are two options: trademark the name before someone else does, or buy it from its owner—and then trademark it. Here are four variations on the theme:

Trademark it. Salon.com is a San Francisco-based Internet media company with revenues of $6.3 million. As its founder, David Talbot loved the domain name Salon.com, but so did a man in Texas who wanted to start a portal for hair salons. For nearly a year, Talbot had to content himself with a clunky alternative, Salon1999.com, before moving the site to SalonMagazine.com, where it resided for two years. Before an initial public offering, Talbot's vice president, Andrew Ross, negotiated the purchase of the coveted address for an undisclosed sum. Ross's challenger moved his portal site to Salon.net, and Talbot's company now owns the trademark to Salon.com.

Mediabistro.com (formerly Hireminds.com), a New York City job-search site for media people, took a different tack. "I didn't realize—stupidly—that I had to apply for a trademark for the name also," says founder Laurel Touby. "I figured, 'Hey, I'm using the name. I'm safe and set.' "But then a challenger from Cambridge, Mass., applied for the trademark for "Hireminds.com." He also registered such variations as Hire-minds.com, Hireminds.net, and Hiremind.com. "He called me and tried to buy my domain name from me, telling me he basically had all associated names," Touby says. The case was settled; the challenger got the name, and Touby got "several thousand dollars in expenses, lots

41

of heartache, and sleepless nights. But it would have been too costly to go on."

Sometimes, the duel for names ends up as a draw. For example, when HotJobs.com, another job-search site in New York, went to trademark the HotJobs name, it found that two other companies—including one direct competitor—had already applied for it. In the ensuing battle, the Office of Patents and Trademarks declared the terms "Hot Jobs" too generic to be trademarked.

Buy the name. As it was being launched, Eve.com, a women's beauty and cosmetics retailer based in San Francisco, discovered that the URL was owned by Eve Rogers, a six-year-old girl in Virginia. The situation forced company founders Mariam Naficy and Varsha Rao to try reaching an accord with a kindergartner. Rogers's parents mediated negotiations with the retailer but left the final decision in their daughter's hands.

The partners consulted baby-naming books and conducted a study. Eve tested better than any other name. So they tried again, but the young girl balked. Idealab, the company's financier, encouraged Naficy and Rao to persevere. Eventually, they made the girl an offer she couldn't refuse. The ultimate price tag: a family trip to Disneyland, a Compaq desktop PC, $500 worth of merchandise from idealab-backed eToys, an honorary seat on the board for six months, and an undisclosed sum of cash. "Looking back, it's probably one of the best investments we've made," Naficy says.

"Please warn others to purchase their trademark along with their domain name to save themselves a lot of aggravation," says mediabistro.com's Touby.

The bottom line: Search one of the online databases of trademarks to make sure no one has a prior claim to your URL (for more information, try the U.S. Patent and Trademark Office at **www.uspto.gov**). Then file for a trademark as soon as you come up with the domain name you want. An added bonus: Trademarks can be used as collateral in gaining a bank loan or line of credit. (The mark's value is usually equal to your revenues.) ∎

Case 3

Addresses: Making Second Choice Fly

We knew the domain we wanted and put it on the registration application," says Shawn Carpenter, sales and marketing director at Sonnet Software, a $2.5-million company in Liverpool, N.Y. The company assumed that it would be able to register "sonnet.com." It assumed wrong.

Doug Bray, a technical staffer, asked Sonnet's Internet service provider (ISP) how to file for the domain. The ISP offered to handle it for him. "Normally they charge $50 for it," he says. "But since we signed a few years' contract with them, they waived it." A representative at the ISP—Dreamscape Communications, in Syracuse—did a quick search while Bray was on the telephone and saw that "sonnet.com" was already taken. Bray was surprised and frustrated. "We had to go back to the drawing board to think of new names," he says.

A few days later, armed with several options, Bray tried again. The company's second choice, "sonnetusa.com," wasn't taken, so Dreamscape quickly filed the paperwork. In two weeks, Sonnet was officially awarded the new domain.

To help promote its online presence and build awareness of the somewhat awkward URL, Sonnet printed up business cards that list information for "Sonnet Online," including the company's e-mail address, Web site URL (**www.sonnetusa.com**), and traditional address and phone number. Carpenter says that getting the word out immediately helped publicize the domain name. "We took the cards right away to our first major trade show, and we got a lot of hits after that."

Carpenter admits that it probably hurts Sonnet not to have "sonnet.com" as a domain. "I know some customers have taken a guess at our e-mail address and sent questions to 'sonnet.com,'" he says. But the business cards have made a difference. "They got the 'usa' out there." ■

Case 4

Making Your URL Ubiquitous

"We really came on strong, making sure our Web address is on everything," says Nora Songer, marketing director at Cattron, a small industrial equipment manufacturer in Sharpsville, Pa. Cattron has had a promotional Web site for five years. After the push to include the site's URL on all printed material, the company noticed a corresponding boost in traffic. "A lot of our vendors were surprised and pleased by it," says Songer.

The company sends out 36,000 pieces of direct mail each year and buys four space ads in trade journals each month. Along with traditional information such as phone and fax numbers, the company's URL (**www.cattron.com**) goes on every ad and mailer. It's also on every employee's business card and is featured in the company's listing in various buyers' guides.

A potential buyer might not go to the trouble to fill in a direct mail response card, Songer figures. But that same person browsing the Web might remember later that Cattron has a Web site. "They can go on and not worry about having to answer a bunch of survey questions or being interviewed over the phone," she says, citing reasons why many potential customers don't call or return mailers to companies for information.

Another reason Cattron publicizes the company URL is for international customers. "Our offices are only open from 8 a.m. to 5 p.m. That means people on the West Coast are not going to be able to contact us at 5 p.m. their time," she says. "But if they have a question, they can look at our Web site and send us e-mail. We've had people from Europe and the Far East look at products on our Web site. During their business hours, they can get the information they want." ■

Case 5

Listing with Search Engines

Alan Klotz debuted his photography gallery's Web site in August 1993, but Alan Klotz/Photocollect didn't list with the search engines until October. "Yahoo! wasn't going to review us more than once, so we wanted to be absolutely ready," he says. If his site wasn't ready or didn't impress Yahoo!'s editors, he would have missed his chance to be listed there.

Klotz also listed his New York gallery's site with other search engines, including InfoSeek, the only one that asked him for a fee. "We didn't pay it," he says. "They didn't enforce it." Because so many search engines are on the Web, it's likely that InfoSeek would shrink its listings if it insisted on fees.

To list on each search engine, Klotz visited its Web site and filled out a quick online form. Each registration took about a minute, and Klotz selected his own keywords to classify his site. Afterward, he tested a few by searching on his chosen keywords. He wasn't pleased by what he found. "If you type in 'Photocollect' as a keyword, it finds us immediately," he says. "But if you type in 'photography,' it brings up thousands of entries."

That's the problem many companies face and the reason that Web developers are always trying tricks to ensure their clients' sites pop up first on searches by common keywords. "I'd advise companies to list with the search engines," Klotz says. Not listing is equivalent to opening a store but not listing in the Yellow Pages. "Just be aware that they're slow and overworked. It's hard for them to keep up with the Web's growth." Klotz now uses WebPromote.com (**www.webpromote.com**). For $795, the service keeps Photocollect's name on 100 search engines and 200 bulletin boards.

Klotz's site (**www.photocollect.com**) has been very successful. "We've sold expensive things, which is a shock. We've sold prints for up to $10,000. Plus, we're currently tracking down prints for about 25 hot leads." ∎

Case 6

Siting Your Information

To keep Internet surfers coming back to your Web site, put useful information there and keep it updated. Why? On the Internet, content is king. If traditional advertising is 90% persuasion and 10% information, effective Internet marketing is the opposite: 90% information and 10% persuasion.

Elliott Rabin, president of Ridout Plastics (**www.ridoutplastics.com**), has successfully built an Internet presence with this principle in mind. He created his Web site with $199 in authoring tools and began posting Ridout's entire corporate research library, along with information about the custom-designed plastic components and displays manufactured by his $10-million San Diego company.

Rabin then promoted his site and the information it hosted by listing it with all the major search engines. He spent about five hours a week requesting links with other sites related to plastics and connected with several universities doing research on plastics.

Now, Ridout is *the* plastics Internet site. During the first eight months following its Web debut, 15% of Ridout's new business came from people who first encountered the company on the Web. Since then, the site consistently gets at least 500,000 hits each month. In March 2000, for example, the Web site attracted 23,000 unique customers. The site increased sales of his brochure holders by 50% with no additional marketing efforts, and it led to major contracts with national clients such as State Farm Insurance.

"Fully 25% of our business now comes from the Internet. It's hands down the best marketing tool the company has ever had," says Rabin. With business expanding into 20 new countries, he believes his Internet efforts will continue to pay off. ■

• Case 7 •

Quick Game Gets 'em to Click In

"We were looking for interactive things to put on the site," says Durward Williams, director of sports marketing at Eurosport, a Hillsboro, N.C., soccer equipment cataloger. The $50-million company had always strived to create interesting copy in its print catalog to draw readers. It wanted to do the same when it set up a Web site (www.soccer.com).

Eurosport came up with an interactive feature called "Are You Baggio?," named for Roberto Baggio, one of the world's best soccer players. The feature works like this: Visitors fill out a seven-question survey, selecting their position, temperament, and skill level in soccer. A moment later a screen displays a photo and short essay about the professional soccer player that best matches the visitor's profile. Truly bad players are matched with a Eurosport manager.

"It's definitely drawing people to the site," Williams says. Eurosport's service provider, Catalogue.com, tells the company that most of the site's 2,000-plus daily visitors come to the site from searching soccer players' names on search engines. Visitors who go to the Baggio feature from the home page must scroll past articles about products and soccer players, along with links to the product catalog. Thus, Eurosport has created a flow through its site, much like some retail stores that put the most popular items in the back of the store.

When the company created the Baggio game, it intended to include descriptive fields and perhaps some humorous quotes. But because there was deadline pressure to have the game ready in time for the Web site's debut, the feature was kept fairly simple. "Now I think that's a good thing," says Williams, noting that even visitors with slow modems can play the game quickly. "A quick feature like this can draw visitors back to your site again and again." ∎

Content

Case 8

Bells and Whistles: Fun vs. Function

On the Web, bigger and bolder are better. That's what Rick Edler, who sells real estate outside Los Angeles, figured. Three years ago he ventured onto the Web with a low-tech site—basically, a glorified business card for the Edler Group.

Edler soon saw that some unlikely businesses were building "really cool sites" packed with snappy multimedia features. Just what he needed. "I love gadgets," he admits. So he hired a Web developer who promised to deliver the latest, snazziest technical gimmicks. "We were going to dazzle everyone with all the technology, all the flash," Edler says.

The site they built pulsed with color and motion. Graphics spun all over the screen as testimonials from happy clients scrolled up and down. Edler even threw in movie listings. His first site had cost $285. This one cost $7,000. But it took too long to download. Traffic was disappointing. Those who did visit didn't stay. "So much was happening," Edler says. "You just stared at it like you were watching a commercial. We were scaring people away."

Then the outside Web master disappeared. Edler was appalled to learn that he wasn't authorized to make changes on his own site. He couldn't even update property listings. "I was just completely up the wall," he says. "We'd really lost control of our thing. It was embarrassing. People were calling us about listings that sold two months before."

Edler finally wrested back control of his site and scrapped it. For $2,000, he built a new, simpler version. It has links to Realtor.com and Bamboo.com, where buyers can check listings or take a video house tour. No more razzle-dazzle. "We try to put as much information out there as possible through third parties," Edler says. The feedback has been extremely positive.

Moral of the story? "Keep it simple," stresses Edler. ■

Case 9

Buzz Lures Repeat Traffic

Want visitors to return to your Web site? Create buzz. Healthshop.com, a seller of wellness and natural products, generated buzz—and built community—for just $7,500. The company set up Healthcam, a round-the-clock broadcast of the life of 29-year-old "Dani" as she dieted and exercised to peak condition for her upcoming wedding. Healthshop.com set up video cameras in Dani's office, kitchen, and family room and fed the tape directly to its site. Thousands of visitors logged in repeatedly to e-mail Dani encouragement, read her online diary, and describe their own health struggles. "People were addicted to this thing," says Healthshop.com CEO Glenn Zweig.

Repeat visitors also respond to personalization, which Healthshop.com is doing on a budget. Customizing its own vitamins, like the online mega-retailer GreenTree Nutrition, is too pricey. But, for just a few thousand dollars the company developed HealthPlanner, which transforms a customer's personal data into a complete vitamin, diet, and exercise regimen. ■

Case 10

Disc Jockey Tunes In to Online Lessons

Not many radio stations have listeners from Antarctica to Zaire. DiscJockey.Com does. It's an Internet music network that "broadcasts" over the World Wide Web. No matter where you are, if you have a computer with speakers and a sound card, you can hear nonstop music from 88 different channels—from love songs to zydeco.

Sound like the product of a giant corporation? Hardly. DiscJockey.Com consists of five people holed away in a small office suite in Salem, Mass. With a daily listenership of 175,000, the shoestring operation grew by piggybacking on new technology distributed by larger companies and parlaying one business into three.

Owner Richard Chadwick began his sole proprietorship as a DJ at wedding receptions. In 1995, he posted a Web site to attract bookings. Soon other DJs and bands asked him to design sites for them, so he started doing business as Media Management.

To distinguish himself from other designers, Chadwick looked for a way to embed audio clips into Web sites. He found his solution from RealNetworks, in Seattle, the biggest player in the online audio software market. That's when he realized he could broadcast music over the Web.

Several stations in major cities were already "Webcasting" a duplication of their broadcasts. Chadwick thought, "Why not let the listener choose the kind of music he or she wants to hear?" So in 1997, Chadwick launched DiscJockey.Com with his recently hired coconspirator, Norman Hawley. The duo started with three channels: Top 40, '60s, and '70s. But they realized they'd have to maintain an edge over two other Web music companies—Spinner.com and NetRadio.com—both founded by well-funded media companies. So when RealNetworks released the beta version of G2 ("streaming technology" that greatly improved the sound of Internet audio), DiscJockey.Com immediately licensed it. "RealNetworks was giving the G2 player away free to any Web surfer," Chadwick explains. "If it caught on, millions of people would be able to hear superb audio."

Chadwick and Hawley rapidly configured dozens of channels to support G2 and kept RealNetworks apprised of their progress. Enamored with the pair's enthusiasm and novel application, RealNetworks noted DiscJockey.Com in its online newsletter, which boasts 750,000 subscribers. Within a day, DiscJockey.Com's listenership tripled. "I saw the beta G2 player," e-mailed C.G., a listener from Copenhagen. "Then I found DiscJockey.Com and liked the quality of the transmission."

"The following week," says Chadwick, "they featured a DiscJockey.Com button on their 'showcase' site, which provided a direct link to our site. We had another spike in listenership." By September 1998, 110,000 G2 players were being downloaded daily, and DiscJockey.Com was riding the wave. In a sense, Chadwick says, "we cobranded the G2 technology."

The piggybacking didn't stop with G2. DiscJockey.Com displays the title and artist of each song that is playing and offers a direct link to CDNow, one of the largest online music stores, which gives DiscJockey.Com a percentage of the referral sales.

After only a year, banner ads on DiscJockey.Com accounted for 30% of Media Management's revenues, which were about $230,000 in 1998 (another 50% came from ongoing Web-site design and hosting, with the rest generated by a side business involving recorded phone messages). The "station" accounted for almost all the growth in Media Management's 1999 revenues, which more than doubled to nearly $500,000.

Besides piggybacking and co-branding, DiscJockey.Com offers these lessons for outmaneuvering bigger competitors and growing quickly:

React quickly. "Our competitors didn't adopt G2 as quickly or widely as we did," Chadwick says. "Because we were among the first, RealNetworks promoted us. That made us look big and helped our image with advertisers."

Stay on the cutting edge. "Being the first to put new ideas out there will keep you ahead," Chadwick says. For example, DiscJockey.Com offers three "live" channels where listeners can make requests and send dedications, which are usually played within 5 to 30 minutes. Chadwick says no other Web broadcaster offers this level of interactivity.

Establish key partnerships. It took Chadwick weeks just to find the right person to talk with at CDNow about a deal, and it took weeks of polite, but dogged calls and e-mails to arrange the partnership. "They told me," Chadwick remembers, "that 'the traffic on your site isn't quite at the level we usually require, but we like your spirit.'"

And surprise them. Chadwick says, "I put an audio message on our site that says, 'We're proud to be a partner with CDNow.' I played it for them over the phone. They loved it. It made us look progressive, which set us apart."

Take small, inexpensive steps. "We got a lot of Web design business first," Chadwick says. "Only then did we try a radio station. We started with only three preprogrammed stations. As they succeeded, we added more. Then we added three live request stations. Each time, we did a small test and listened to feedback. We never took a large monetary risk." ■

Case 11

Web's Next Killer App: Arugula?

A host of cyber-entrepreneurs and Internet innovators are convinced that, just as the online arena has changed the way we communicate, shop, and invest, it will change the way we eat. "People have to eat three times a day, but nobody has found a way to get more free time," says David Hodess, CEO and cofounder of Cooking.com, one of the new players catering to today's time-starved consumers.

What to have for dinner tonight? The next five nights? That dinner party you've scheduled for Saturday? Both Hodess's Cooking.com, in Santa Monica, Calif., and another online start-up, Tavolo, in San Rafael, Calif., offer thousands of gourmet products and wares that can help answer those questions. Each site is as much an information resource as a culinary e-tailer. You can click on either site's weekly menu planner for week-at-a-glance menu suggestions, with printer-friendly recipes.

Both sites also offer various bells and whistles. Tavolo's site has features that convert recipes from standard to metric measurements, tailor recipes to the number of people being served, and create a shopping list based on your weekly menu. Cooking.com has an online glossary for boning up on the history of cognac or determining the precise definition of a zapotilla.

But customizable recipes and online glossaries are just the marketing bait. What the sites really aim to do is sell products. "Providing a free recipe certainly has value for the consumer," says Ken Cassar, an e-commerce analyst with Jupiter Communications, an Internet consulting company in New York City. "But it's also a great opportunity to sell mortars and pestles."

As Tavolo founder and CEO Kevin Applebaum is fond of noting, with $55 billion in total sales (both online and on terra firma), the market for cooking products and gourmet foods represents a huge category. The leading national retailer of cooking supplies—Williams-Sonoma—has a market share of less than 1%. But Applebaum, who honed his marketing skills at PepsiCo and Procter & Gamble, also knows he's not alone in spotting cooking sites' potential. Numerous national retailers are also chasing the ever-expanding online opportunity.

The real challenge for all the gourmet sites, says Michael May, another Jupiter Communications analyst, will be to get the people who purchase gourmet food and wares online to go from buying gifts to buying for themselves. The majority of the $200 million in online sales of small appliances and gourmet-food items in 1999 occurred during the fourth quarter, for holiday gifts, notes May. Arugula-artichoke-with-roasted-garlic pesto pasta sauce may make a terrific gift, but it isn't what people are buying for their own dinner tables—at least not tonight. ■

Case 12

Not Every Business Begets a Cult

Daniel Harrison is an early adopter if there ever was one. Poolandspa.com (formerly Paramount Services)—his Long Island, N.Y., pool and hot-tub supply—was on the Web even before Amazon.com. Back in 1996, chat rooms and message boards were becoming centers of passionate customer interaction, focusing on products as diverse as electric trains and knitting yarn. "We thought such a community would work for us," Harrison says.

Harrison's ISP agreed to install chat technology on his site in April 1996. Poolandspa.com would pay a $2,500 outlay for the software, and the ISP promised to provide free service after it was up and running. "We were really excited," Harrison recalls. "We put notices on our main pages that next Wednesday we were going to have a live online chat with our customers at 10 p.m., and we offered 10% off products bought during the chat."

Come Wednesday, Harrison and five of his servicemen stayed after hours to run the chat. They were sure they were going to be swamped with inquiries. Unfortunately, they were barely outnumbered. "We had maybe 10 people come," notes Harrison.

The crew was happy anyway. The technology worked. Poolandspa.com was again on the cutting edge. Harrison figured that the weekly audience would grow to 30 quickly, then shoot upward. But only six showed up for the second go-around. And week three was quieter still.

Harrison realized his mistake. "If the hot-tub water is turning your kid's hair green, you don't want to wait for the answer until Wednesday night at 10," he says. "My customers don't want to talk to each other. If they have a question, they want to talk to an expert." ■

Case 13

Sell Yourself with Your Signature

On the Internet, where massive amounts of information compete for users' attention, you need "secret weapons" to let people know about your products and services. Case in point: BookZone, which bills itself as "The Net's Largest Publishing Community." To become the leading provider of Internet services for book publishers, the folks at BookZone (www.bookzone.com), one of the oldest book sites, based in Scottsdale, Ariz., used the lowly "signature."

An e-mail signature is a file that contains a small text blurb that automatically attaches to the end of your e-mail messages. It allows you to add information about your company, services, and products without having to retype it every time you send an e-mail or post a message to a newsgroup. This addendum helps spread the word about your offerings without actually selling. You can mention a special sale, promote a client, bolster your benefits, or float a fresh idea, even if your message doesn't talk about your business at all.

Mary Westheimer, BookZone's CEO, not only mentions her company's services, she also changes her signature daily to promote BookZone's clients. Sales for those publishers have risen as much as 75% on the days their latest book titles are part of her signature.

"Signatures are easy to use, but people generally don't know about them," says Westheimer. "E-mail is so powerful. It's easy to do, and it works well. It's an obvious strategy, but I'm always amazed because for every person who uses a signature, I meet four or five people who have Web sites but don't use signatures. They're one of the easiest and most powerful ways to market on the Internet." ■

Case 14

Retailer Retools Its Competitive Edge

Back in 1994, Robert and Karen Ludgin were worried about their company. Coastal Tools, in West Hartford, Conn., had been selling mid- and high-range tools, primarily to professional contractors for over 12 years. But business had peaked in the early 1990s, and even more threatening, the big home-improvement warehouse chain Home Depot was coming to town.

But then the Ludgins hired Todd Mogren to update computer systems at the 10-employee company. Mogren focused much of his energy on the Internet, achieving impressive results. He launched the Coastal Tools Web site in 1996, with an initial budget of $2,000. Being there first was key. Because there were virtually no other tool sellers on the Internet at the time, the site (www.coastaltools.com) attracted plenty of customers. Being on the Web also offered several marketing advantages, including customer convenience, greater reach, and wider access to the niche market of professionals that buy Coastal's products.

"We thought we could do maybe $100,000 worth of tools on the Internet that year," says Mogren. "We ended up doing about $188,000." Sales jumped to $887,000 in 1997, $1.5 million in 1998, and $2.95 million in 1999. (The portion of total sales the figures represent remains confidential.)

The company's technology investment has grown as well. Coastal now spends between $75,000 and $100,000 advertising its Web site and recently invested $100,000 in an inventory-management and order-processing system. Still, Mogren says the site has been paying for itself since it was launched. And amazingly, the site has changed little from its original design. The only significant difference was the addition of a "shopping cart" feature in the second year, making it easier for customers to select multiple items.

However, the company's Web experience has not been problem-free. The order processing system was not installed in time for the Christmas 1999 season, creating delays for a handful of customers and headaches for staff members. "If you disappoint people on the Internet, they don't tell 10 people, they tell thousands," Mogren says.

Apparently, there's no need to worry about fallout. Sales for the first few weeks in 2000 ran roughly 50% ahead of the same period in 1999. Better yet, on the strength of its Internet sales, Coastal Tools moved to a much larger facility in West Hartford—just across the street from Home Depot, a competitor the company no longer fears. ∎

Case 15

Web Sites Work for Mom and Pop, Too

While it's unlikely that small stores with chiefly local constituencies will make major international sales on the Internet, even the most basic Web sites give retailers a chance to serve their regular customers better, insists Jim Sterne, president of Target Marketing, in Santa Barbara, Calif.

Simply posting street address, phone number, hours of operation, and directions is useful to customers who prefer to shop in person. A Web site is also the perfect place to advertise specials or to promote industry-specific tie-ins. A small vitamin store might include an e-mail link to a pharmacist, for example, so customers can ask questions without picking up the phone.

Three or four basic Web pages can cost nothing at all through sites such as Xoom.com (www.xoom.com) or only about $20 a month to reside on AOL's server. To promote small local sites, Sterne suggests listing your Web address in the Yellow Pages and on the Web sites of local chambers of commerce, which generally offer free listings.

The Herb Shop, in Boca Raton, Fla., for example, has a no-frills site that lists phone number, street and e-mail addresses, and some product information. Ordering online is not an option, but customers can call in or e-mail their orders. Within several months, the shop made an extra $10,000 in sales from its site, mostly to out-of-state customers. Owner Kathy Dodds pays a local vendor $130 a month to host and update her site, which the vendor developed for free because she was its first customer. ∎

Marketing

Case 16

E-newsletter Clicks with Buyers

Sunbelt Software (**www.sunbelt-software.com**), in Clearwater, Fla., develops Windows NT systems management tools. The 75-employee company produces a weekly e-mail newsletter, *W2Knews*, whose information-rich content reaches a whopping 600,000 system managers and other target readers. New readers sign up for free subscriptions at the rate of 250 a day.

While daily traffic at Sunbelt's site runs about 3,000-plus, it soars to 10,000 to 15,000 right after a new issue of *W2Knews* goes out. "About 5%—30,000—of subscribers are buyers," says president Stu Sjouwerman. "We spent $3,600 a month on servers and a double T-1 line for the newsletter, and it helped drive $13 million to us in 1999." ∎

Case 17

Target Marketing via E-zines

Although the Internet as a medium is relatively new, the same print or direct-mail marketing rules still apply: When online, market to a target audience. Jim Daniels points to the response of an ad he ran for his company, JDD Publishing (**www.bizweb2000.com**), in Smithfield, R.I., in two online newsletters. Newsletter No. 1 had more than 250,000 subscribers, and the response was three times that of Newsletter No. 2. Even so, Newsletter No. 1 resulted in only two sales. Newsletter No. 2 had a subscription base of only 8,000 but resulted in eight sales.

Why were the results so different? The smaller publication was read by people interested in business-opportunity products.

Daniels notes that the number of quality e-zines (online magazines) is growing at a rapid pace, so finding five or six related to what you are selling should be relatively easy. An e-zine listing of almost 4,400 electronic 'zines can be found on the Web at **www.meer.net/~johnl/e-zine-list**. ∎

Marketing

Case 18

Banner Exchange: Test for Free

Want to drive traffic to your Web site? Cash-strapped entrepreneurs can advertise their sites for free by exchanging banner ads—those 1- by 5-inch digital billboards. The concept of free banner exchange is not new, but the process has gotten easier through matchmaking services such as SmartAge (**www.smartage.com**) and LinkExchange (**www.linkexchange.com**).

Since it's not always easy to measure the number of sales you get from banner exchanges, success boils down to three basic rules: Make sure your ad is engaging, swap with sites that complement your business, and don't expect the moon.

Banner exchange worked for Deborah Edlhuber, owner of Prairie Frontier, in Waukesha, Wis., which sells wildflower and prairie-grass seed. Edlhuber erected a Web site in early 1997, chiefly as a marketing vehicle. Within a few months, she contracted with LinkExchange to place her self-created ad on several dozen gardening and photographic sites. Today, the site (**www.prairiefrontier.com**) attracts up to 2,000 hits a day, many from visitors clicking over from Edlhuber's LinkExchange partners.

"The banners definitely bring people to my site, and I can track the click-throughs," she says. Her one caveat: "It's still hard to say how much business I get from them." ∎

Case 19

Nightclub Swings with 100-Page Site

Alberto's Salsa Studio & Nightclub has a Web site (www.albertos.com) that is a glimpse of the future of online marketing. The $1-million dance club is in Mountain View, Calif., the heart of Silicon Valley, where most of those employed work for high-tech companies with unlimited access to the Web. So when owner Alberto Martin runs an ad or promotion for his club on his Web site, thousands of people see it, and hundreds go to the club.

Although such a response is still limited to the few geographic areas that have high percentages of consumers using the Web regularly, in the future, running an ad on the Web will be as common—and effective—as buying space in a local newspaper.

Martin opened his Web site more than six years ago. Because he was his ISP's first customer, he was able to negotiate a low price—$100 a year—at a time when the Web was still in its infancy. The ISP doesn't maintain or make changes to the site; Martin does that himself once a week, sometimes outsourcing it to a developer.

The site itself is about 100 pages, including directions to the nightclub, pictures of the room, and fun features like online salsa lessons. The main element is a simple event calendar. Every month, a new calendar lists all upcoming musical artists and special parties. Martin makes attending these events more compelling for Web visitors with his special online promotions. For example, the nightclub frequently offers discounted cover charges to patrons who e-mail their reservations by a certain date. The customer gets a return e-mail to print out and take to the nightclub as proof that the lower entry fee applies. Martin also started offering special e-mail-only parties.

"We didn't know what kind of response we'd get," he says. "I figured a few people would come." So he waived the cover charge the first few times.

The second time he offered it, he got 200 responses from people coming to the 300-person capacity club. Now the twice-monthly nights are so popular that there's a cover charge, but it's lower for patrons with a printout of the invitation from the Web page.

"We got rid of our print mailing list," Martin says. Instead, he uses his 3,000-name electronic mailing list to keep patrons updated on upcoming events, saving $1,500 per month in printing and mailing expenses. In 1997, Martin started marketing to specific groups on his list. When he sees a lot of e-mail addresses from a particular company, like "intel.com," he contacts the company about holding a special party at the nightclub. The company nights soon triggered a good chunk of additional business.

Being able to leverage his electronic mailing list means that Martin saves on traditional marketing expenses. "We used to do more radio promotions," he says. "That can cost you $200 for 30 seconds. We've been able to cut the radio budget by two-thirds by advertising salsa nights exclusively on the Web." That's about $1,000 per week.

Martin was also able to quit printing and handing out flyers to promote events. "It's hard to tell who looks at your print ad," he says. But tracking reports from a Web site can effectively trace how many people look at the site and for how long. He promotes the Web site on all of his traditional marketing material. "The URL goes on our business cards—every piece of paper we have," says Martin.

What's next? Martin hopes to add more entertainment to the site, such as live music shows and video dance lessons. "We're small compared to other companies on the Web," he says. But he figures being small is an advantage. "We can do things pretty quickly." ∎

Case 20

Selling Links to Your Site

"We get zillions of people e-mailing us and asking for links," says Kate Heyhoe, editor of the Web's *The Global Gourmet* (TGG, formerly *electronic Gourmet Guide*), an electronic magazine about gourmet cooking. Located in Crestline, Calif., TGG (www.globalgourmet.com) currently uses The Kitchen Link (www.kitchenlink.com), which maintains some 10,000 links. "It saves us money. It's expensive to maintain those lists," says publisher Tom Way. "Our policy is that we don't automatically do mutual links." (Mutual links go from TGG to another site and from the other site back to TGG.) Many Web site administrators trade links with compatible sites without charging for them. TGG, however, makes money on those deals.

"Web-site linking is valuable," Heyhoe says. "And we bring more to a lot of sites than others out there, so we don't pay—we expect people to pay us."

When another site administrator—say, from a cooking utensil catalog—calls Heyhoe to ask if TGG is interested in linking to the catalog, the first thing she considers is the site's value. How many users regularly visit the catalog? Is it a broader audience than TGG draws on its own? Is it the target audience that TGG strives to reach? This type of information is available from a site's tracking or hit-rate reports. Second, Heyhoe looks at the quality of the other site. Is it easy for users to get back to TGG, or will TGG just be sending them away? Does the site take too long to load onto the computer? "We've branded TGG and want to keep the image as a responsible site with top quality," Heyhoe says.

If the answers fit TGG's profile, the company strikes a deal with the other site, charging it a monthly fee. Many Web sites trade mutual links without charge. Those that do charge a fee levy anywhere from a few hundred dollars a month to a few thousand. ∎

Case 21

Giving Birth to National Sales

Many of Liz Lange's friends became pregnant at about the same time, and had nothing kind to say about the maternity clothes on the market. "My friends were all telling me that they couldn't find anything normal to wear," says the 33-year-old former *Vogue* fashion editor. She investigated the complaints and says, "I was pretty horrified by what I saw—baggy tops and big bows." So, in 1997, she started a company aimed at selling stylish maternity wear. Then Lange herself became pregnant and had a son in 1998.

In founding Liz Lange Maternity, Lange sought to retain fashionable styling while adding the comfort of new stretch-knit fabrics. She set up a small shop in a New York City office building, showing her 10-piece sample line by appointment. Within a month she was working "round the clock," she reports. Because time is always an issue for pregnant women, Lange hooked up with a factory that could complete orders in two weeks. Soon, orders were pouring in.

Lange then launched an Internet-marketing site (www.lizlange.com) because, she explains, "it was the fastest, cheapest way to get pictures of my clothes across the country." In February 1999, she opened a 650-sq.-ft. boutique in Manhattan and began work on a print catalog that was soon offered free through the Web site. Business boomed, and in March 2000, Lange opened a 3,000-sq.-ft. store on Madison Avenue.

With revenues of more than $2 million in 1999, and online buyers throughout the country, Lange says that her business took off "in a way that I never could have imagined." Her next goal is to open more retail stores in other cities, such as Los Angeles. ∎

Case 22

Web Acrobatics

How do you make your most current marketing materials available to customers and partners immediately, in full color, with virtually no fulfillment costs? Just convert your data files into Adobe Acrobat portable document format and post them on your Web site.

That's how Sequencia (formerly PID Inc.), a $10-million company in Phoenix, conveyed its batch-automation software marketing information to its *Fortune* 500 customers. Robert Hylton, former director of marketing for the company, used Adobe Acrobat (www.adobe.com) to compress large graphic files of marketing pieces into smaller files that anyone could read with Adobe's free Acrobat Reader software. Customers who filled out a short prospecting survey could download the files immediately from Sequencia's Web site (www.sequencia.com). Or, Hylton e-mailed the files to key customers, distributors, and employees worldwide.

In the first six months after the files were posted on the site, about 2,000 prospects downloaded Sequencia's marketing materials. Those leads brought 20 qualified prospects into the sales process, which, Hylton estimates, brought more than $1 million in sales. ■

Case 23

Clocks Click on Antique Network

Ken and Susan Markley, proprietors of Old Timers Antique Clocks (**www.antiqnet.com/oldtimers**), in Camp Hill, Pa., joined Antique Networking (**www.antiqnet.com**), an online mall that includes some 250 antiques dealers who photograph their wares with digital cameras and post the pictures on the site. In return for just 2% of sales and $50 a month, Antique Networking displays the Markleys' clocks on its site, which receives 3 million hits a month from 90 countries.

In 1999, customers from as far away as Singapore bought 244 of the Markleys' clocks through the network, and Ken reports that their business has increased 60% in the two years they have been affiliated with Antique Networking. ■

Case 24

Setting Up Shop in a Cybermall

When Julie Bridge set up a Web site for Personal Creations (www.personalize.com), her gift catalog company in Burr Ridge, Ill., she chose the Evergreen Internet Cybermart mall to create and maintain it. What impressed her most was that Evergreen had already landed the catalog giant, Spiegel. "We were really looking for someone who had experience with a catalog company," says Bridge, whose sales top $20 million. "Some developers we spoke to hadn't even done online sales."

Bridge found Evergreen by cruising the Web and noting which developers had built sites for the major catalogers. She signed a six-month nonexclusive contract with Evergreen, specifying that if she leaves the mall, she can take all elements of the site with her to a new mall or server company, except for the online sales capability. She paid $4,700 for a 31-page site, including $900 for use of the transaction software. Evergreen adds pages at a cost of about $100 per page, which includes scanning in graphics and the company logo. Bridge also pays $12.50 per page per month as "rent" in the mall. In return, Evergreen forwards customer e-mail from the site and makes text changes. Bridge currently uses WebOrder by Smith-Gardner (**www.smith-gardner.com**).

The anchor store concept pays off for Bridge. "Somebody comes in to see Spiegel and decides they want to see what our site is about," she says. Of all visitors who stop at Personal Creations' site, 70% come from outside the mall, and 30% come from within. "Those 30% never would have seen our site if we had opened up shop outside the mall," concludes Bridge. ∎

Case 25

Add Cybervalue to Your Proposal

Even if you're not in the Web design business, offer your Internet skills to new customers—and your company may benefit. Paul L. Berg, former CEO of Enterprise Builders, a midsized construction company in Simsbury, Conn., not only knew a lot about building structures, he could also build Web sites.

When bidding on a job to build a private school, Berg discovered that the school needed to raise funds to pay for the construction. So, he included free Web-site design and hosting services in his bid. Berg explained that the site could be used for fundraising and showing alumni and contributors the results of their generosity. When school officials saw he had their interests in mind, they awarded him the contract. This added value made his proposal stand out from the competition.

It cost Berg $9 per month to rent space from a local Internet service provider and $100 to register his client's domain name. He spent one weekend designing the school's site, and half an hour every month to update it with the photos of the building's progress. The Web site accomplished two goals: It attracted funds for the school, which were necessary to pay Berg, and it showcased his construction work, both on location and on the Internet.

Creating the Web site also helped Berg discover his true calling; he is now CEO of Applied Technology (**www.paulberg.com**), also in Simsbury, providing Internet marketing and Web development consulting services. ■

Case 26

Dreamboats Set Sale on the Web

When Tom Neckel, Sr., and four partners bought Sumerset Houseboats in 1996, the company was already the nation's leading builder of houseboats—in this case, luxurious versions of those shallow-draft motorcraft used primarily on inland waters. Despite being an industry leader, the Somerset, Ky.-based company had a few problems.

In particular, there was no way to communicate effectively with customers. Sumerset circulated CAD diagrams of the boats to its customers through the mail, but few customers were able to read the schematic diagrams properly.

When buyers arrived to pick up their vessels—which can cost upwards of $200,000—they often were surprised by particular construction elements, says Neckel. The kitchen might be smaller than they expected. Or they may have missed the location of a set of stairs leading belowdecks. The builder could make after-the-fact alterations, but this led to customer dissatisfaction, which Neckel feared would dampen important repeat business. The last-minute fixes also led to morale problems among employees.

Neckel, who bought out his partners in January 1999, decided the solution was to provide customers with pictures of their boats *while they were being built.* The best way to do this, he realized, was via the Internet. So, Sumerset launched a Web site (www.sumerset.com) in February 1997, at a cost of about $16,000. "Initially the site had the feel of a brochure," says Neckel. "But we soon realized it had to be interactive to accomplish our goals."

In early 1998, the company began posting in-progress photos of each of the 16 or so boats then under construction. The photos, which are now standard procedure, begin with the early-stage welding of the hulls and continue through cabinetry and finish work. Sumerset also uses its Web site to host

Support/Feedback

periodic online chats, allowing customers to pose questions to specialists in the areas of safety, financing, or the complexities of boat delivery.

Back in 1996, Neckel had envisioned reaching international customers—there was one at the time—inexpensively via the Web. Today, 10% of the 150-odd boats built annually are sold to foreign customers, and roughly 40% of all visitors to the Sumerset Web site come from outside the United States.

The site has also had some unanticipated benefits. The assembly line moves faster now that workers know photos of their progress will be posted daily. Sumerset also stopped staffing the two-week long Miami boat show when surveys revealed that every new customer who attended the show had already visited Sumerset's Web site. "That's $100,000 [a year] that went directly to the bottom line," says Neckel.

Sumerset now sells about 10% fewer boats, but customers are trading up. Repeat business has risen from 40% to 70%, and the average price of a boat has risen from about $135,000 to $208,000. In 1999, revenues approached $29 million—double the 1996 figure.

"We estimate that by the end of 2000, we'll be a $50-million company," says Neckel, with justifiable pride. ∎

Case 27

Add 'Net Value for Customers

At Balentine & Co., a midsized investment firm in Atlanta (**www.balentineonline.com**), combing the Internet for hard data gives the company a customer-service edge. Its consultants bolster their investment advice with information they've pulled off the Internet.

Gary Martin, for example, was the first to start passing along key information to clients. He had lunch one day with a client who mentioned that he was thinking of developing a design for a plastic wheelchair, but wasn't sure how to gauge market interest. Martin offered to browse the Net for the client, to see if he could turn up any leads.

And turn them up he did.

Using a few keywords, Martin quickly found a newsgroup for people with disabilities and posted a message asking users for feedback on the idea. Within a few weeks, Martin had heard back from enough users to be able to pass along encouraging news to his client: Most of the respondents had three wheelchairs in different locations and found the prospect of one lightweight portable chair very appealing.

Today, it's a given: Intelligence gathering on the Internet is one of Balentine's basic client services. ■

Support/Feedback

Case 28

Community Builds Repeat Business

Among its more traditional services, Idyll Untours, a 20-employee travel firm in Media, Penn., also finds short-term rental housing in residential neighborhoods for overseas travelers. The firm hosts an online community (**www.untours.com**), which enables customers to offer tips and answer one another's travel questions via e-mails that are accessible to all.

Idyll spawned its online community—which is self-sustaining and growing—by informing its 4,000 clients by mail of the community's existence. The firm paid $400 to develop the site, but the cost is only $45 per month for a local Internet service provider. An Idyll employee spends half an hour a day acting as host, plus some time on offline administrative tasks.

Marilee Taussig, an online community consultant with The Ruth Institute, also in Media, and daughter of Idyll owner Hal Taussig, estimates that the online community is responsible for one-third of Idyll's repeat customers. ■

Case 29

Tracking 3,000 Visitors Daily

Windham Hill Records, in Beverly Hills, Calif., is one company that watches Web-site traffic closely. Within three months of opening, the $30-million record company's site (**www.windham.com**) logged 300,000 visitors. That number now stands at about 91,000 per month.

When Windham Hill started looking for tracking software, Brett Cohen, senior manager of strategic marketing, was particularly interested in what type of tracking reports were available. Since the company planned to use the information as a guideline for promoting particular artists, he wanted it to be as reliable as possible.

Windham Hill uses InterShop Merchant Software to track individual Web-site visitors. Each week, Cohen looks at a summary and overview of how many visitors there were, the average time each spent at the site, what sections they visited, and for what length of time. Based on that feedback, Windham Hill has redesigned the site twice since its debut.

Although the company wants the site reports to be as informative as possible, it does not insist that visitors register to access the site. "They don't want to be reminded that they're being overtly tracked," says Cohen. ∎

Case 30

Promoting in Newsgroups

It was a new customer who told William Houde-Smith, of LaserMax Inc., that his product was a hot topic in one of the Internet's newsgroups. A police officer called to place an order for the company's gun laser sights and mentioned that he'd found out about the product after posting a question in a newsgroup about guns. The day after his post, the policeman had received more than 80 messages about the Rochester, N.Y., company.

Houde-Smith started reading the messages that were posted in the newsgroups that his customer had recommended. In one message, a person asked how one of LaserMax's products worked. "I posted a non-hype kind of response," he says. "I knew enough Internet etiquette so I didn't flog the product. I focused on the product concept and ideas."

"I was amazed about the discussions about our products," he says. "There are a lot of philosophical issues among people who use our sights." Houde-Smith makes clear that he's from LaserMax, but he says it doesn't bother people in the newsgroup that he has a commercial interest. "They appreciate the fact that I'm an industry expert."

The group Houde-Smith regularly visits has a resource section that lists LaserMax's Web address (**www.lasermax-inc.com**). "It helps to have someone regularly monitoring the newsgroups and contributing to discussions there," he says. "The newsgroups are like fishing nets that direct people to the Web site." ■

Case 31

Need Opinion on New Item? Go Online

Bite Shoes, a manufacturer of golf shoes in Redmond, Wash., was set to launch a new model, the "Reverse Pivot." But since the shoe incorporated some nontraditional features and because producing a new shoe is a pricey proposition—about $50,000 per style—Bite Shoes founder Dale Bathum felt he needed some input. However, he didn't want to pay for a formal focus group or for flying in buyers from all over the country. So he held what amounted to an informal focus group and queried golfers and buyers—online.

The company posted a photo of the new shoes on its Web site (www.biteshoes.com), then e-mailed 50 loyal customers and 10 top buyers for pro shops. The e-mails referred recipients to the site and asked them questions about the shoe's style and price.

Based on 60 responses, the golfers liked the shoe and even asked for more color options. But "the store guys didn't like it—they just didn't want to take the risk," says Bathum. And since the company doesn't yet sell online direct to customers, the buyers' preferences prevailed. Bite Shoes scrapped the Reverse Pivot and decided to focus on developing more golf sandals, which generate about 45% of the company's revenues.

Besides cost savings, Bathum plans to continue using the Internet for informal focus groups for an additional reason—the high-quality contact. After receiving e-mail responses from buyers, Bite Shoes' reps can follow up by phone. "You have a reason to call them up, other than trying to sell them something," says Bathum. "Plus, they feel as if they're part of the process." ∎

Support/Feedback

Case 32

Web Widens Legal Boundaries

As demand for skilled labor grows, an increasing number of employers need help recruiting foreign workers. But immigration laws regulating permanent and temporary visas are confusing and complicated. Enter attorney José Latour, president of José E. Latour and Associates, in Gainesville, Fla., an online law firm that provides legal immigration compliance services (**www.usvisanews.com**). For example, the firm has a Canadian client, a marine construction contractor that operates shipyards in the United States. "Shipyards are in tremendous need of skilled marine engineers," notes Latour. "By using our e-mail system and our Web site (to educate prospective hires), we helped that client place dozens of engineers from Canada in its U.S. shipyards."

In 1997, with only 10% of his clients hailing from Florida, Latour realized that he was running ragged trying to communicate in traditional "low-tech" ways. So he invested $50,000 in a Web site and e-mail. The firm recouped the initial investment quickly when its Web site netted a $100,000 account in early 1998. "I knew the Internet would be an economical tool for correspondence and transfer of information," says Latour.

Having an online presence also facilitates customer service. Latour says his staff of 10 answers all e-mail and phone messages—around 800 per day—on the same day they are received. "Law firms don't talk about customer service much," Latour continues, "but it's the one major factor that has led to our growth." ∎

Case 33

Useful Info Gets Site Seers to Sign In

"We realized that the Web was not just an advertising medium, but really an interactive medium," says Lisa Courtney, former head of the online department at Busey Bank, in Urbana, Ill. "People using it wanted to communicate, to put something in and get something back." By offering visitors a game as an incentive to register at the site, Courtney accomplished two important goals: Visitors got a chance to interact and play, while the bank gathered demographic data on those visitors.

Within six months of opening its Web site (www.busey.com), the $12-million bank formed a separate department for online strategy. "Initially, we viewed the Web as something very separate from banking," Courtney says. "Then it became more involved in our overall marketing strategy." To monitor the effectiveness of Web marketing, the bank used a software package called Illustra to track how customers moved from page to page through the site, and what path they took before signing up for one of the bank's services.

To make that tracking information more meaningful, Busey also wanted to gather basic demographic data from visitors in a short registration form. But unlike many other Web sites, Busey didn't demand that all visitors register before they accessed the site. Instead, the bank encouraged visitors to register by offering useful information in return. "We didn't want to make coming to the site restrictive," Courtney says. "Hopefully, we offered something of value so the visitors wanted to register." ∎

Support/Feedback

Case 34

Freebies Entice Surfers to Sign On

The number of visitors to your site is increasing. So how do you get them to register so you can transform them into sales leads? Corporate consultant and author Floyd Hurt, of Floyd Hurt & Associates (**www.rousingcreativity.com**), in Charlotte, Va., is in the business of corporate creativity, so he's always looking for creative ways to get business people to register on his site. "Our biggest success has been with a free subscription e-mail containing a creativity tip of the week. Subscribers love it, and it keeps them coming back," says Jim Henerberry, who bills himself as the company's vice president of intergalactic sales.

Other ways to generate registration? Take a survey or offer to answer questions or give free advice. Better yet, use the oldest method in the book—give something away for free. It can simply be a free report. It doesn't have to be a product.

Henerberry is also careful not to ask for too much. "We only ask for e-mail addresses at first." And it doesn't hurt to remind Web-site visitors that their personal information will not be sold. "For us, it's about dialogue, not list building," he says. ∎

Support/Feedback

Case 35

Giving Consumers Five Ways to Buy

"My goal is to get paid," says Robert Olson co-founder of wine.com (formerly Virtual Vineyards). "It's not my goal to invent new technology." The online wine retailer's Web site (www.wine.com) offers several ways for customers to make purchases: mailed checks, faxed orders, e-mailed credit-card orders, encrypted credit-card orders, and purchases made via the CyberCash transaction service. "The only thing we wouldn't know what to do with is cash," says Olson.

The encryption software is included at no charge in wine.com's Netscape Commerce Server software. When customers who use a Netscape browser send any message to the company, the message is automatically encrypted by the browser software and then unencrypted after it arrives at wine.com's server. The CyberCash option is free to merchants. CyberCash charges banks that process the transactions and consumers when they make a transaction.

Although he offers these options, Olson says 75% of its orders now come via encrypted messages. Even though it has a firewall, wine.com doesn't store any credit-card numbers on its Internet server. "We'd have a public relations disaster if someone stole our credit cards," Olson says. "A lot of merchants don't understand that this is where the risk is."

"There's no standard for online sales right now," he adds. "And it's not clear why any merchant should seek one. They should be independent of loyalty toward one type of transaction option." Olson compares online transactions to traditional retail transactions, for which most consumers have a walletful of credit cards from which to choose. "Why be a store that limits customers to only one of those payment methods?" ■

Case 36

E-commerce Recipe Evolves Over Time

When Ben and Donna Nourse cooked up a business plan for greatfood.com (www.greatfood.com) in 1996, the term *e-commerce* was as fresh as a warm baguette, and specialty food suppliers were telling the husband-and-wife team they'd never make it selling mustard and croutons on the Internet.

Still, the founders applied plenty of expertise to their Seattle-based venture, which was bought out by 1-800-flowers.com in November 1999. As vice-president of merchandising, Donna drew on years of experience in the food industry to choose good suppliers and delectable offerings. As president, Ben brought to the table business development experience and a knack for technology. (He's now a nationally recognized expert on Internet commerce.) Today greatfood.com, which employs 35 people, makes money from commissions received from the makers of 1,500 specialty food items it sells online.

But greatfood.com's e-commerce success didn't come merely from being one of the first Web retailers. "It came from evolving the site with new features and deeper content, and by continually changing the business's approach to marketing and relationships," says Ben. Here are some lessons in evolution from the veterans behind "the ultimate site for gourmet consumers, wholesalers, and gift buyers."

The Nourses' first decision was to invest in expensive, high-end e-commerce software instead of building the site's technical capability themselves. They used the first version of Netscape's Merchant System for handling credit-card transactions and for grabbing data from an industrial-strength Oracle database containing all of greatfood.com's product and customer information. All they needed to add later was regular hardware upgrades, plus Macromedia Dreamweaver for HTML editing and Macromedia Fireworks for manipulating Web graphics.

As soon as they went "live," the Nourses encountered their first major challenge: keeping the site looking fresh and inviting for both new and repeat visitors. "We decided against animation because it was too bandwidth-intensive for our customers, many of whom log on with 28.8 bps modems," says Ben. "Our objective is universal access, so we tend to stay away from leading-edge technologies." Instead, design improvements make the site attractive and easy to navigate, and enhanced content builds customer affinity.

"I believe if you're not doing a major redesign a couple of times a year, you're not doing your job," says Ben, who hired a full-time graphic artist to design—and redesign—the home page and keep underlying pages consistent and compelling.

To bring repeat business, the Nourses added two new categories in 1998: *Gift Finder*, which suggests gifts for different occasions and price ranges; and *Meal Occasions*, where shoppers can order specialty foods grouped for everything from tailgate parties to romantic dinners. A continually rotating menu of new recipes, tips from visiting chefs, product reviews, and features on entertaining keep greatfood.com simmering. "We are great believers in the value of editorial content. We want our customers to come to our site with questions about food, even when they're not interested in purchasing," Ben says.

Another way to build affinity is through personalization. Currently, the Nourses are experimenting with "dynamic Web pages," created to match the visitor's history, profile, or preferences as he or she logs in. A lover of chocolate, for example, may be greeted with a special on a box of truffles, while a salsa aficionado would see a layout on Habañero peppers.

Even though consumers were flocking to their site, the Nourses wanted to make greater inroads with two profitable segments: commercial accounts and corporate gift buyers. They did so, again, through a deft mix of fresh design and added content.

"We added tabs on the site to make it easy for these users to go directly to the content they desire," said Nourse. Corporate gift buyers, for example, can consult an etiquette checklist that outlines when it's appropriate—and when not—to send gifts. Wholesale buyers can return often for information on new brands, industry news, and even the addresses of competing suppliers.

With the explosion in the number of Web sites, the Nourses now compete with dozens of gourmet food sites, resulting in a new challenge: getting noticed. "In the early days, the main objective was to get the major search engines to index your site, then you were sure to get reviewed. But now there are just too many sites," says Ben. Greatfood.com attacks the problem through partnerships, sponsorships, and non-electronic media.

Since banner advertising did not generate quality visitors, they are driving traffic to the site through two networks of online partnerships. Their first informal program, patterned after Amazon.com's, was so successful that in 1999 the Nourses formalized it as the greatfood.com Affiliate Program and brought on a full-time program manager. Today, a healthy percentage of the site's 500,000 monthly visitors are generated through several hundred greatfood.com affiliates, each of whom receives a 10% commission on any greatfood.com sale generated through its site.

Sponsorships are also attracting notice—and new customers. "We pay a fixed fee, for example, to sponsor the gourmet grocery area of Excite Shopping," said Nourse, who has inked similar deals with Yahoo!, America Online, and Peapod.com, an online grocery store.

Looking back, Ben says, "There's more pressure today to create a Web business instantly. We were lucky in that we had a chance to build a business plan and develop our relationships slowly." ■

Case 37

How a Hot-Sauce Shop Sells Online

In late 1994, Perry and Monica Bosserman Lopez opened a Web site for Hot Hot Hot, their 300-sq.-ft. hot sauce specialty shop and catalog in Pasadena, Calif. By early 1996, the Web site was bringing in 24% of the store's $300,000 in retail and catalog sales. Govind (Ben) Arora, vice-president of Internet operations, reports that the company then closed its retail store in early 1997, and 91% of sales now come from the Internet, while catalog orders account for 9% of sales.

The 25-page site (www.hothothot.com) is a burst of colorful computer graphics and hot-sauce labels. All 225 products are online. "We had to categorize them," explains Perry Lopez, "otherwise it would be overwhelming. In a shop, it's not so intense because there's more room." Visitors to Hot Hot Hot's Web site click on pictures of the sauces they're interested in and can read about where the sauce is from, its ingredients, and its heat level. "On the Web, your selling tools are limited to text, graphics, and information flow," Monica Lopez says. "Ours is a food product, and customers can't touch or taste it. It becomes more an issue of providing information to create a need or desire for the product."

Customers who want to buy an item click on that option. A software program written by Brave New World, the company's Web developer, tracks the orders so that when the customer goes to the order pages, all the chosen foods and sauces are listed automatically. The customer can then either print out the page and fax it to the store, call Hot Hot Hot's 800 number, or e-mail the order form with a credit-card number. The small company couldn't afford encryption software (which secures online credit-card orders) when the site debuted, so the Lopezes decided to try sales without it.

Although many industry analysts warn that consumers are afraid to shop online, Perry and Monica haven't found that to be true. When the site first opened, about half of the online orders came over the phone and half via unencrypted e-mail. Now e-mail orders are up to 80%. The shop receives and processes about 18 orders a day from the Web site.

Usually at least one of the daily orders is from an overseas customer, which initially surprised Perry and Monica. "You're instantaneously a global company," Monica says.

When Perry started exploring the idea of a Web site, he knew that their tiny retail shop couldn't afford to set one up in-house. So when Web development company Brave New World (BNW) approached him, he struck a deal with the startup. BNW, also in Pasadena, charged $20,000 to create the site, with Hot Hot Hot paying that off as a percentage of online sales. The retailer continues to pay BNW $225 a month for about an hour each month of ongoing site maintenance, including design changes.

Selling online is more profitable than selling via catalog, with its high printing and mailing costs. Processing e-mail orders is cheaper than paying for a toll-free order line. But getting customers to find the site and then return to it is tough. And the fact that the customer is the one who initiates and drives the sale is a big challenge, which Hot Hot Hot handles by providing a captivating site with lots of product information and interaction.

"The store is a totally personal experience—customers can see, touch, smell, and taste what they are going to purchase. The salesperson is much more an active character," Monica explains. "There can be a real detached quality to ordering by computer, so it's important to respond to customer e-mail. These customers want to know that you are really there."

Among the benefits of a strong site, she adds, is that one online sale usually leads to another. "On the gift-card orders, they write, 'Can you believe we ordered this from the Internet?,' which is great word of mouth." ∎

Case 38

Branding Is Fine, but Selling Is Better

NetGrocer.com founder Uri Evan launched his Web-based grocery business in North Brunswick, N.J., in 1997. Evan planned a groundbreaking, brand-building site. Customers who came to his home page would first learn all about the company and its mission. Then they could click down to do their grocery shopping.

A 63-year-old techie, Evan built the tech infrastructure and raised capital for his online venture. In the months after launch, the company was ready to charge into an initial public offering. But there were signs of trouble. NetGrocer struggled to convert its traffic to sales. Also, $1.3 million was tied up in inventory, shipping expenses were high, and NetGrocer was operating deeply in the red. In September 1998, the planned IPO was scuttled at the last minute. Evan and his board asked Fred Horowitz, one of the company's angel investors, to become its interim CEO.

Horowitz didn't know all that much about the Web, but he did know how to sell groceries. He had helped to build a $240-million laundry-detergent manufacturer in the 1980s. "Freddy placed more of an emphasis on retail and merchandising than the original team, which was more computer and systems oriented," Evan says.

Maybe Horowitz wasn't a Web-slinger by trade, but he could see that NetGrocer was going about its business all wrong. The problem was symbolized by its home page—a tasteful opener that laid out the company's mission. The new CEO thought the genteel welcome was a lot of garbage. Customers had to click through level after level of the site before they could buy anything. Web or no Web, if you want to sell groceries, you have to get the product in front of the customer—right on the shelf, as it were.

Today the revamped site is an unabashed hard sell. It bombards visitors with pictures of products, coupon offers, and "click to buy" links. "Every supermarket can hang 20 or 30 posters near the entrance to provide information about the deals they're offering," says Evan. "That kind of merchandising was missing from our original site."

The redesign created a spectacular turnaround. The average order size jumped by 20%. Repeat customers typically spend $60 an order. And the company's conversion rate—the number of people who check out the site and then actually buy something—almost tripled. "It was a dramatic improvement," Horowitz says. "If you can get conversion, you have the foundation for a successful business." ∎

Case 39

Lessons from the Links

Without the Web, Tom Cox, president and CEO of Golfballs.com (www.golfballs.com), a golf-ball retailer with 20 employees, based in New Iberia, La., wouldn't even have a company name. With the Web, he holed more than $1 million in sales in 1999—up from $250,000 in 1998. Based on his experience, Cox explains that there are four secrets to doing business on the Internet:

Provide a high level of customization. "The trick to making people feel loyal to your site and return consistently is to personalize it," says Cox. "Make it not so much a mass medium as a 'me' medium." Golfballs.com sells just about every type of golf ball imaginable, but if you want to buy a rare ball not offered, Cox will find it for you. If you need special software to track golf scores of different golfers on different courses, you'll find it in the Golf Links section. Want to determine the right kind of golf ball for your particular game? Try Golfballs.com's interactive program. Want a catalog without divulging all your personal data? Type in your e-mail address, and a catalog will be in your mailbox minutes later.

Target a niche that others can't touch. A target audience can be made up of people who like rare golf balls, but *women* who like rare golf balls is even more closely targeted. With women accounting for 20% of all golf purchases, Cox is building new areas on his site for that market.

Focus your product or service. Above all, to succeed on the Web, you need to focus on providing a single item at great prices. "What works best is a single focus—whether it's books, wine, or groceries," stresses Cox. "Take one thing and offer it at hard-to-beat prices, with a wide selection no bricks-and-mortar competitor could fit into a physical space as easily, and combine it with quick shipping."

Boasting an unbeatable inventory and discounted prices, Golfballs.com offers 1,200 varieties of balls from leading names such as Titleist, Greg Norman, Flying Lady, Viper, and Hole in One (average order: $60). The company also sells used balls and X-Outs—balls with slight imperfections, such as a number left off—at a substantial discount. Even better are Logo-overruns, brand new golf balls with a random company's logo on them.

Prime the pump with freebies. Among Cox's favorite gimmicks for encouraging repeat business is a "Balls and Caps" giveaway. "It costs us about $30 per week," he says, "and we get roughly 200 to 300 participants per day" who enter online for the weekly drawing. Cox estimates that the giveaway accounts for 20% of the Web site's hits (which often total 80,000 to 100,000 per day) and produced at least 5% of the company's 1999 revenues.

You've got to adopt the attitude that the Web is strategically important to your business, advises Cox. "Electronic commerce isn't rocket science," he says. "It's much more important than that. Everything you do should be geared toward making customers stick around long enough or come back often enough to make a buying decision." ■

Case 40

Party of 10? Click Here

Sure, much of the online cooking sector caters to aspiring chefs. But what if you and the kitchen aren't on speaking terms? And you happen to like it that way?

Take heart. A crop of new sites seek to gratify the pantry-phobic as well. Feel like takeout tonight? San Francisco-based Food.com offers online ordering—and, more important, local delivery—from more than 13,000 restaurants nationwide. Feeding your face is merely a matter of entering your zip code and navigating menu offerings. Since restaurants are notoriously low-tech, the company's server in Seattle translates online orders into a fax or a phone call, which is then sent to participating eateries, a service for which Food.com reaps a $400 setup fee, a $50-a-month retainer, and 5% of each order.

For those who'd rather dine out, at least two new companies offer on-line reservations. Both foodline.com, in New York City, and OpenTable.com, in San Francisco, are attempting to replace the traditional phone-and-paper-based restaurant-reservation system with a Web-based one. They charge participating restaurants about $200 a month in service and transaction fees (and in OpenTable.com's case, a $1,000 setup fee). Currently serving a handful of cities, both plan to go nationwide and to ultimately link their service directly into the restaurants' individual point-of-sale systems. They also hope to personalize the diner's experience. "Imagine being able to remember that Mr. Jones is allergic to shellfish or sending a promotional e-mail to your top 100 August diners," rhapsodizes former lawyer Paul Lightfoot, Foodline.com's 29-year-old CEO.

CookExpress.com, launched in January 1999, offers an online option that's between cooking from scratch and dining out: a gourmet, ready-to-cook meal sent to your home by FedEx. Founder Darby Williams, 46—another Microsoft escapee—calls CookExpress.com a "smarter way to cook." Three-part meals (for example, roasted salmon with herb-caper sauce, potato-olive salad, and baby arugula), each requiring less than 30 minutes to fix, are delivered to your door (currently just in the Bay Area, where CookExpress.com is based) or by overnight delivery nationwide. Prices range from $8 to $15 per serving, plus a single $4.95 local delivery charge or a shipping cost of $12.95 to $16.95 (based on the number of meals).

Yeah, but is the stuff fresh? To mollify those squeamish about the idea of filet mignon that arrived through a delivery service (albeit packed in high-tech gelatin ice), the company has devised a system of labeling each package with color-coded dots that change color if the food hasn't remained chilled. The packaging also indicates how long the food inside should stay fresh (usually two days).

Williams boasts that the company has the potential to be a billion-dollar enterprise within five years. He plans to expand the CookExpress.com same-day service into at least 30 U.S. markets as well as another 6 to 8 markets outside the United States—each worth $25 million in his estimation. He also hopes to add a retail component to his distribution.

The logistical complexity of such an undertaking actually appeals to Williams, although, he readily concedes, "had I been in the food business before, I probably never would have done this." ■

Case 41

To Grow Sales, Think "Niche Knack"

A Web site can greatly widen your customer base. But how do you set your site apart from those posted by hundreds of similar companies? Specialize and become interactive.

That's the advice of David Brough at J.P. Faddoul Co., a giftware shop and bridal registry in Shrewsbury, Mass., that has sold china, crystal, and giftware for 35 years. In 1998, when Brough decided to create a Web site (**www.jpfaddoul.com**), he specialized—offering a simple interactive service that helps people find replacement pieces for discontinued patterns.

A visitor enters the name of a piece and pattern in a brief online form. Brough checks his own inventory and industry sources, then responds by e-mail. The customer can order a found piece by phone or fax. Of course, customers sometimes buy other items and tell friends about Faddoul, so now Brough gets orders from across the country.

"The key is to make the site interactive," Brough says. The form and a long list of patterns "also make us look bigger than we are. No one would guess this business is operated by just me, my mother, and grandmother."

Brough contains the cost of his site by taking a do-it-yourself approach and by avoiding full-blown e-commerce (customers do not make purchases online). The site cost $1,500 to start; hosting and upkeep costs run $60 a month. Brough, who took a local course on how to use the Internet and how to build Web pages, does the work himself. He spends only a few hours a week maintaining the site, and two full days responding to inquiries. With that, "Our orders have doubled," he says. "We haven't hired anyone, and the actual shop is only open four days a week." ■

CyberSpeak

Baud When transmitting data, the number of times the medium's "state" changes per second. For example: a 56k baud modem changes the signal it sends on the phone line 56,000 times per second.

Bits per second (bps) The speed at which bits are transmitted over a communications medium. (Note that Bps is *bytes* per second.)

Browser A software package that allows you to access the Web.

BTW Common abbreviation in mail and news, meaning "by the way."

CIX Commercial Internet Exchange; an agreement among network providers that allows them to do accounting for commercial traffic.

Cybercash Another word for e-cash (electronic cash). Electronic money.

Cyberspace A mystical intersection of people and technology on the seemingly infinite network.

Dedicated line See leased line.

Dial-up To connect to a computer by calling it up on the telephone. Often, "dial-up" only refers to the kind of connection you make when using a terminal emulator and a regular modem.

DNS The Domain Name System; a distributed database system for translating computer names (say, tinker@AOL.com) into numeric Internet addresses (e.g., 264.35.71.2), and vice-versa. DNS allows you to use the Internet without remembering long lists of numbers.

Domain name An Internet identifier for e-mail addresses and Web locations. Domain names are registered by Network Solutions Inc., under its Internet Network Information Center (InterNIC). Top-level domain names include: .com (commercial businesses); .org (nonprofit organizations); .net (networks); .edu (educational institutions); .gov (government agencies); and .mil (military). Currently, more than 80% of the Internet names represent "dotcoms."

E-cash Electronic cash. Coming to a computer near you: a functional electronic banking system that will enable you to use electronic cash to transact business online.

Electronic mail A messaging system that lets you communicate electronically around the world for the price of a local telephone call (in many places) plus the cost of your Internet access provider.

FAQ A frequently asked question, or a list of frequently asked questions and their answers. Many USENET newsgroups maintain FAQ lists so that participants won't waste a lot of time answering the same set of questions.

Firewall A form of computer security that protects proprietary information from being accessed from computers outside the organization.

Flaming Transmitting highly negative and damning information about an individual, company, or organization. People who write flames are known as "flamers."

FTP File Transfer Protocol is a method for delivering ordinary text information over the Internet. It allows you to download a file from, say, the Library of Congress, to your computer.

Hit The number of times a file on a Web page is requested by a browser (vs. *impression*, which is the number of times a file is downloaded by a user or visitor).

http Hypertext Transfer Protocol is a mechanism for delivering hypertext, or multi-dimensional, information over the Internet.

Hypertext Information linked in a web structure on a computer allowing all works referenced in a particular work to be instantly accessible. Hypertext links can be graphical, video, and/or audio in addition to text.

Internet The "Net" is a global library and discussion center in cyberspace. As the "network of networks," it is an aggregation of computer and information networks.

InterNIC Internet Network Information Center (see *domain name*).

IP Internet protocol.

Leased line A permanently connected private telephone line between two locations. Leased lines are typically used to connect a moderate-sized local network to an Internet service provider.

CyberSpeak

Modem An electronic unit that connects a computer to a data transmission line (typically a telephone line). Most users now rely on modems that transfer data at 56k (56,000) bits per second (bps) or more.

Navigation bar A set of buttons, words, or graphic images (typically in a row or column) used as a "click" link to major topic sections on a Web site.

Netiquette Internet etiquette.

Newsgroup Any collection of posted messages on a specific topic found in USENET. Also known as online discussion group.

Search engine Online software that helps you navigate the morass of information on the Internet.

Shareware Proprietary software that can be freely copied (a.k.a. *freeware*). Some shareware products provide payment incentives, such as updates and support.

Signature A file, typically up to five lines long, inserted at the end of electronic mail messages or USENET news articles. Besides a name and an e-mail address, signatures usually contain a postal address, slogan, and logo or other graphic element.

URL An acronym for "Uniform Resource Locator," URL is an address for the exact location of information on the Internet.

USENET A large, informal collection of newsgroups that exchange "news" similar to "bulletin boards" on other networks. USENET predates the Internet, but these days, the Internet is used to transfer much of the USENET's traffic.

Web browser Software that enables you to find and read information on the Web.

Web server A computer linked to the Internet that serves up information in the form of text, graphics, and multimedia. Any computer can be turned into a Web server by installing server software and connecting it to the Internet.

World Wide Web The World Wide Web is a particular location of information on the Internet. Often confused with the Internet, the Web is only one section of the online universe. Its major technical asset is the ease with which it supports hypertext.